# COLETTE
*The Difficulty of Loving*

# COLETTE

## *The Difficulty of Loving*

### A Biography

*by*
*Margaret Crosland*

PETER OWEN · LONDON

ISBN 0 7206 0302 1

PETER OWEN LIMITED
12 Kendrick Mews Kendrick Place London SW7

First British Commonwealth edition 1973
© 1973 Margaret Crosland

Printed in Great Britain by
The Garden City Press Limited Letchworth

B. COL
484,031

To Dr L-S

# Contents

# *Illustrations* (between pages 76 and 77)

The day will come when people will 'psychoanalyse' Colette. May it not bring us truths which are too disappointing, mingled with over-pretentious mistakes! In the meantime let us be content with the outside. It is full of sap and savour; it does not lie. Mistrustful sceptics will ask: Is this a true portrait? The answer will be: Ask Colette; and she may not know. In any case, it is in harmony with her work. Even if it offers us a half-legendary Colette, let us console ourselves: it is the Colette that will endure, and therefore it is the real one.

PIERRE TRAHARD

*Paris, 1941*                                            *L'Art de Colette*

# Foreword

When I first wrote about Colette in 1953 I had the rare pleasure of meeting her in the famous Palais-Royal apartment. We talked, or rather she talked, not of books but of cooking, knitting, embroidery. Since that time I have read and re-read her books, discussed them and tried to separate, both in her life and her writing, fact from fiction. This double problem will perhaps only be solved when Professor Claude Pichois, scrupulous editor and annotator of Colette's letters, is able to complete his careful research and eventually publish the full-length study on which he is now working.

The centenary year of 1973 will probably bring new material and memories to light; our picture of Colette may well be modified, but since her books give her immortality, the picture will only be deepened and enriched, never invalidated. In the meantime I have tried to show how Colette's character and life gave her writing its particular slant and flavour. There will always be controversy about it. For instance, while some of the books, notably parts of *La Maison de Claudine*, are recommended reading for school children in France, Colette's reputation, distorted by rumour and tinged with scandal, has frightened off many people who, although they have never read her books, assert that they are lesbian and immoral. The richness, the vitality, the sheer quality of Colette's marvellous observation (of all living things,

11

from human beings to butterflies and plants, and of non-living things like houses, which she brought to life), unfortunately passes them by. It is their loss.

'I belong to a country I have abandoned', wrote Colette in one of her sincere if melodramatic moments, regretting her care-free childhood in the Puisaye, near Auxerre. Since then her work has reached many other countries; there is much interest in her in Germany, both of a popular and academic sort, even if some of her books have been banned in Spain. In the U.S. there has been curious homage : photographs of her have been carried through the streets by 'women's lib' demonstrators and a kind of musical comedy about her life was produced off Broadway, later making a brief appearance in Britain. Films, radio plays and television programmes based on Colette's work have been made in several countries.

In her work there was a strange opposition between the un-conscious artistry which so quickly became professional, and the conscious if often disguised theatrical conceptions behind the writing. The characters in her novels confront each other as though on a stage, while short articles are planned with the care-ful rise and fall of a piece of music. I believe that the woman who was described by her last husband as 'the least' literary person' he had ever met, was not aware of any difference between the 'real' and the 'unreal'. She was in one sense wholly literary, for she had become literature during her lifetime. I believe too that Colette's love of drama and the theatre was a major element in her life and work; it has never been easy to separate the woman from the actress. When she was nearly eighty she interrupted a conversation with me, picked up a hand mirror and said with apologetic dismay, 'I forgot to put any rouge on.'

Many people have given me invaluable help in the prepara-tion of this book. I owe much to Professor Pichois and the other writers listed in the bibliography, who have all contributed to research and interpretation relating to Colette. I would also like to acknowledge the personal co-operation I have received from Colette's daughter, Madame Colette de Jouvenel, and from Monsieur Maurice Goudeket; among the many other people I would like to thank are Monsieur Armand Avronsart, Miss Elizabeth Berridge, Bryher, Madame Adry de Carbuccia, Madame Lily Denis, Madame Jeanne Durand of Flammarion, Mademoiselle Odette Evezard, secretary of the Société des Amis de Colette en Puisaye, the librarian of *Le Figaro*, Mr Graham Greene, Mrs Penny Harper for showing me her thesis on Colette and the theme of the 'earthly paradise', Frank Hauser of the Oxford Playhouse Company, Mr R. D. Hewlett, Head of Reference and Research Services, BBC, Miss Jean Mauldon, Mrs Beatrice Musgrave, the library staff of *Paris-Match*, Madame Pauline Tissandier and Miss Antonia White.

Quotations from *La Maison de Claudine* are from, or based on, the translation by U. Truebridge and E. McLeod published as *My Mother's House* by Secker and Warburg, London, 1953. Some essays included in the English volume *Places* (Peter Owen, London, 1970) and passages from *The Evening Star* (Peter Owen, London, 1973) are quoted from the translation of David Le Vay. Thanks are due to the various copyright owners for permission to quote from Colette's books and letters.

*London*, 1973                                           M.C

# Introduction: Colette s'en va

'August for the people, and their favourite islands' : a Paris August is quieter than most, the streets are filled only with tourists because many of the offices, shops and restaurants are closed. The newspapers rarely contain any news and if they do, there is no one to read it. In early August, 1954 one news item occupied many daily papers and illustrated magazines. Colette was dead. At the end of January that year she had been eighty-one; photographs showed her in the Palais-Royal apartment which had become a legend – the triangular face had become slightly fuller, the shrewd eyes seemed harder, yet more distant beneath the cloud of mauve hair. Other photographs pictured her at lunch in the apartment with her husband, Maurice Goudeket, or being carried in her wheelchair into the plane which was to take her to stay with Prince Rainier of Monaco. Her last major book of the fifty or so she wrote had been published in 1949, two minor ones appeared the same year and by 1950 Flammarion had published the Le Fleuron edition of her complete works in fifteen volumes.

'Death,' she had written, 'does not interest me. Neither does my own death.' She saw death only as the end of life, of no importance, causing no fear. In *L'Etoile Vesper* she had described a dream which seemed to forecast this end of living, caused

15

finally by cardiac failure. Her friends believed that she died simply because she no longer had any wish to live.

Many people mourned her, for in those fifty or so books there was, to use a cliché, something for everyone : university teachers, the well-read middle-class, the concierge herself, schoolchildren, and the literary critics, something for the young, the middle-aged and the old. All her life Colette had attracted a large public, and a great deal of publicity, even if the two were not necessarily inter-related, and both had been acquired by accident.

Literary critics hastily prepared their farewell articles and some hoped they might soon have an opportunity to say something about Colette that was more interesting, if not necessarily less laudatory, than mere ecstasy or nostalgia. Before they could write much, however, an unexpected controversy broke out.

It had perhaps been assumed that Colette, President of the Académie Goncourt and a classic in her lifetime, would be accorded a national and religious funeral. The Cardinal-Archbishop of Paris, who had been away on holiday, decided that someone who had been twice divorced and had not received the last sacraments could not be buried according to the Catholic rite. For the first time in French history a woman was granted the honour of a state funeral, but the Church took no part in it. In compensation, perhaps, it was very well staged.

A catafalque draped in tricolour was set up in the Cour d'Honneur of the Palais-Royal and perhaps nobody had expected that in this Paris August so many thousands of French people, mainly women, would pass before it in homage. Philippe Hériat, friend of Colette and a fellow-member of the Académie Goncourt, wrote an emotional account of this occasion, comparing it with the 'hardly democratic' pomp that accompanied Valéry and the autograph-hunters who pursued the mourners of Christian Bérard. 'This time it was Paris, Paris in mourning for Colette. The choice of this place, which was an idea coming from the heart, the perfect ordering of the ceremony and its relative brevity after the long file-past, the golden air, at this time when the trees were in full leaf and the horizon clear, the windows with their lowered blinds before which a flock of pigeons . . . unfurled like scarves : everything contributed, all was in harmony.' Hériat, a dramatist himself, mentioned that flowers had come from such different admirers as a music-hall association and the Queen Mother of Belgium, 'and may I reveal the irony of this coincidence? – the purple dahlias from *Les Lettres Françaises* leant against the aristocratic flowers from *Le Figaro*'.

The thunderstorm which broke over Paris after the remaining ceremony at Père-Lachaise might have warned the Cardinal Archbishop of another storm on the way. Graham Greene had come from England to attend the funeral and on 14th August *Le Figaro Littéraire* published an open letter from him to His Eminence the Cardinal Archbishop of Paris, Cardinal Feltin. He stated that Catholics must have found this ceremony 'strangely truncated', for they were used to praying for their dead. He pointed out that everyone who had been baptized a Catholic had the right to be accompanied by a priest as far as the grave, and no one could forfeit this right. 'But today [he wrote], through your decision, no priest has offered public prayers for Colette. Your reasons are known to all of us. But would they have been invoked if Colette had been less famous? Forget the great writer and remember an old lady of eighty who, at the time when Your Eminence had not yet been ordained, made an unfortunate marriage not through her fault (unless innocence is a fault) and afterwards broke the law of the Church through a second and a third marriage. Are two civil marriages so unpardonable?' Some saints had behaved worse, they had repented; who could know how Colette had felt? The Archbishop had condemned her on insufficient evidence. He had given the impression that the Church pursued the guilty after death. Was this an indirect warning against the evils of divorce? The British novelist warmed to his attack as he pointed out that this decision would scandalize intelligent people, and non-Catholics would wonder if the Church lacked charity. A writer whose books we love becomes a being dear to us. 'This is not an abstract case taken from a collection of moral theology for the use of seminarists.'

Many Catholics in France, Britain and the United States would be hurt by 'the fact that Your Eminence, through such a strict interpretation of the rule, seems to deny the hope of this final intervention of grace on which Your Eminence and all of us depend at our last hour'.

The Archbishop defended his decision but the controversy remained so heated that a teacher from the Institut Catholique wrote an article in the *Revue de Paris* setting out in detail the rule of the Church concerning religious burial. *Le Figaro Littéraire* printed many letters and in London *The Times*, which had published an obituary notice of Colette containing several errors, reported that most of the letters received had supported the Archbishop's decision.

A tombstone of black and pink granite, from Colette's native Puisaye, was erected over her grave. Her husband Maurice Goudeket stated in his book *La Douceur de Vieillir* that he would have liked to see a cross on the stone for various reasons, 'and partly, too, because I fear that a day will come when passers-by will no longer know whether it was the Church, or Colette herself, who refused to allow it there'.

Colette's funeral, Colette's 'religion' are still discussed in Paris today. There is also, in certain places, a Colette-religion, and, naturally, an anti-Colette religion. The reality lies somewhere between the two.

# I

## *In Search of Lost Parents*

Since drama seemed inevitable, it would be a mistake to ignore, deny or belittle it. Better to accept it as the keynote to this life and its inseparable work. Whereas the life seems to have been invented by a novelist, the work contains a minimum of invention : its value lies in the treatment. Colette wrote about herself, about what she had done or seen, people she had loved or thought she loved. Loving and writing were the two most difficult things for her, for she found as many problems in her emotional involvement with her parents, husbands or lovers as she found in covering sheets of paper with words in an order that satisfied her. Immense energy and skill allowed Colette to carry out the process of subduing actual events, people and words; after long and almost invisible aggression she achieved in the end a smoothly-running life and a literary style of apparent ease.

When in her old age she was described as a 'legendary figure' it might have seemed that there was nothing more to say. But legend has only cardboard walls, easily demolished, revealing a reality infinitely more interesting. It is known that Colette was born in Burgundy in 1873, that her voice never lost the rolled r's associated with that part of France. In spite of her often-quoted love of good food and wine it would be a mistake to assume that she came of a long line of Burgundian ancestors who had spent their lives in the vineyards. A series of accidents and only

19

partly-understood events brought her parents together in the area of the Yonne known as the Puisaye, a name of Celtic origin which means 'the wooded country'. Her mother came from the north of France, her father from the south, and neither of them had led an ordinary life before they met.

Because of her mother's deep and lasting influence on Colette, admirers and scholars have tried to discover all possible background information – with disappointing results. *La Maison de Claudine,* Colette's principal contribution to the history of her family, contains intriguing details which never cease to challenge anyone with a passion for genealogical research. When writing about her family Colette selected only those details which seemed to her relevant. Objective truth did not interest her and dates were of little importance. It is unlikely that she would have known all the facts, anyway, for her mother was convinced that *her* mother-in-law was a liar.

The admirable research work of Madeleine Raaphorst-Rousseau has shown that Colette's mother's family can be traced back to the seventeenth century, when the Landoys were simple working people at La Neuville in the Marne. The Departmental archives of the Ardennes reveal that a direct ancestor of Adèle-Sidonie Landoy settled in Charleville in about 1787 and ran a grocery business. His son Henri-Marie, who was born at Charleville in 1792, continued the grocery business and *La Maison de Claudine* recounts two interesting details about him – he manufactured chocolate and was 'a coloured man', known as 'the Gorilla'. Colette describes him as 'a quadroon, I believe' and added the details she had seen in a daguerrreotype, which showed 'a high white cravat, with pale, contemptuous eyes, and a long nose above the thick Negro lips that had inspired his nickname'. Madeleine Raaphorst-Rousseau states that in spite of the interest shown by Monsieur René Robinet, archivist at Mézières-Charleville, in Henri-Marie Landoy, research can go no further. There is no trace of coloured blood in the Landoy side of the family, it could have been introduced by Henri-Marie's mother but nothing can be learnt of her (except that her family moved about a good deal) since the parish registers concerned have been destroyed.

The daguerreotype of 'the Gorilla' may have been stolen together with that of his wife, as recorded by Colette, and miraculously found again in a flea-market. Colette also described him, through her mother, as ugly but fascinating. Women found him so attractive that he had a great number of children. Of those born to his wife, Sophie Chatenoy of Versailles, two of the five sons did not survive. His only other legitimate child was a daughter, younger than all the sons, born in the boulevard Bonne-Nouvelle in Paris and baptized Adèle-Sidonie. Her mother died soon after her birth and a nurse was engaged to care for the baby. She was found at a farm in the village of Mézilles, a few miles from Saint-Sauveur-en-Puisaye. There has been speculation concerning the reason for this choice, the most interesting suggestion being that her father and brother belonged to some secret society persecuted by Louis-Philippe's government. The well-wooded area of the Puisaye is said to have been haunted by druids in the past, but in any case it formed a suitable hiding-place for anyone on the run.

'The Gorilla' remarried, went to Lyon and died there in 1854, when 'Sido', his daughter, was nineteen. She was removed into the care of her two brothers, who were much older than she was. According to Colette, they were French journalists, 'married and settled in Belgium', and naturally Sido's friends at this period consisted of 'painters, musicians and poets – an entire Bohemia of young French and Belgian artists'. Little additional information has been found to fill out these few details, for, in writing about her mother, Colette transformed her into a character of her own imagination, simply by ignoring some facts and magnifying others.

We do know that Henri-Eugène, Sido's elder brother, had left a bead factory in Paris to take up journalism, and in 1840 he and his younger brother left France for political reasons, settled in Belgium and after ten years took Belgian nationality. Henri-Eugène was appointed editor of *Le Journal de Gand* in 1863. Sido, then, was no ordinary village girl, even though she had lived for several years on the farm at Mézilles. Evidently she loved country life – and her childhood friends – for she returned to the Puisaye for holiday visits.

It was here that she met her first husband; Colette was the only one to speak kindly of him but whether this was through choice or ignorance is not known. Jules Robineau-Duclos, 'scion of gentlemen glass-blowers', was twenty-one years older than Sidonie Landoy. He owned a great deal of land, farmhouses and other property in the Puisaye and one of the farms, La Guillemette, bordered on the one where Sido's foster-mother lived. Colette described in *La Maison de Claudine* how Robineau-Duclos – known as 'the Savage', because he liked to go out hunting alone – had seen Sido, 'not particularly pretty, but attractive', during a visit to his property, and had been impressed by her wide mouth, pointed chin and humorous grey eyes, her sturdy slenderness. He found it hard to forget her, for she was different from the women to whom he was accustomed, 'his servant-girls, easy conquests as easily forsaken'. Colette went on to show that Sido returned a certain amount of interest : 'The passing vision of this man on his strawberry roan, with his youthful black beard and romantic pallor, was not unpleasing to this young woman. . . .' At some point Colette must have learnt from her mother and acquaintances what actually happened, but the chapter from *La Maison de Claudine,* entitled 'The Savage' has been proved to be a highly romantic version of the events, an unusual type of treatment for Colette. It had not in fact occurred to Jules Robineau-Duclos that he might marry an attractive girl from Belgium. It had not occurred to him to contemplate marriage at all, for he was really only interested in alcohol. In spite of his money and possessions he must have been deeply unhappy for he apparently drank *eau-de-vie* all day. Some of the servant-girl conquests were not 'forsaken' for at least one of them, who had already given 'the Savage' a son, decided that it would be to her advantage to move into the farm where he lived, help herself to what she fancied and perhaps even inherit money and possessions. The Robineau-Duclos family and its related families decided that they must put a stop to this situation.

A wife must be found for Robineau-Duclos and heirs produced quickly. But where could a suitable young woman be found? His reputation was so bad that no local girl would tolerate him. Special legal arrangements had already been made to protect his sister's interests. Fortunately somebody, a certain Monsieur Bourgoint, apparently, thought of the visitor from Belgium. If 'the Savage' was responsible for choosing his own bride he had not lost all sense of judgement, but local research in the Saint-Sauveur area, conducted with great assiduity by the late Emile Amblard, and discussed by Raymond Escholier in *Le Figaro Littéraire*, indicates that everything was decided on his behalf. Since Sido had no parents the request for her hand was made to her brothers in Belgium. It took a week of hard bargaining before the marriage settlement was completed. Sido and 'the Savage' were married near Brussels early in 1857. The bride was twenty-two, with no dowry, the groom was forty-three and if according to contemporary documents he was 'frighteningly ugly', his six farms, woods, property and at least one vineyard made him an acceptable husband.

Sido, one of the most important figures in Colette's life and writing, had no easy introduction to adulthood. First of all she had to brace herself to a total change of atmosphere on all levels. As she grew up she had been, in Colette's words, 'emancipated . . . accustomed to the frank companionship of her brothers and their friends'. Even if her mother's life had not been ideal before her first marriage, Colette found it necessary to make it so. A

23

pity, no doubt, to leave 'the warm Belgian house and the vaulted kitchen that smelled of gas, new bread and coffee; she left behind the piano, the violin, the big Salvator Rosa inherited from her father, the tobacco jar and the long slender clay pipes, the coke braziers, the open books and crumpled newspapers. . . .' The Puisaye, with its miles of open fields, woods, scattered houses and villages was, and still is today, as different as could be imagined from the cosy, casual atmosphere that Sido apparently left behind in Belgium. The house where she came to live was full of surprises, with a white and gold drawing-room, unpainted icy bedrooms, family silver, and cut-glass goblets for the free-flowing wine. Colette's transcription of her mother's life reads as though the stage were set for some sinister opera : 'In the evenings, by candlelight, shadowy old women sat spinning in the kitchen, stripping and winding flax grown on the estate to make heavy cold linen. . . . The shrill cackle of truculent kitchenmaids rose and fell, depending on their master's approach or departure; bearded old witches cast malign glances upon the young bride, and a handsome laundry-maid, discarded by the squire, leaned against the well, filling the air with noisy lamentations whenever the Savage was out hunting.'

If the marriage had been arranged in the hope that there would be an heir for the Robineau-Duclos estates, everyone, including Sido, who longed for a baby, had some time to wait, for three years went by before she acquired one. In the meantime she energetically whitewashed the farm kitchen and instructed her staff in the art of Flemish cookery. Colette writes of these domestic virtues with admiration, telling also how lonely and bored Madame Robineau-Duclos became. She missed conversation, family warmth, and friends. Even the Savage, who had made an effort to restrict his drinking, noticed his wife was sad and apparently rode forty miles in order to buy her a marble pestle and mortar and a cashmere shawl. Sido never forgot his 'first unselfish act', but admitted that it was also his last.

Writing in 1924, some twelve years after her mother's death, Colette gives a carefully selected picture of the man who must surely have made her mother very unhappy. Colette did not intend the dark side of the story to cast its shadow over that almost idyllic book. But dark side there was, for in 1953, in a collection of letters which Colette allowed *Le Figaro Littéraire* to publish was one which revealed at least one alarming incident in Sido's early married life. 'One day Jules Robineau, after drinking, tried to beat me (two months after my marriage). Ah, that was a splendid massacre. I threw at him what was on the chimney piece, among other things a lamp-holder with sharp edges : he received it full on the face and bore the scar from it until his dying day. I was pleased with myself. That taught him better.'

Jules Robineau-Duclos soon returned to the serious drinking he had interrupted only briefly at the start of his marriage. Sido's life at least was made happier when her daughter Juliette was born in 1860 after three years of waiting. She was to develop into a strange girl and Colette herself admitted what the photographs show, when she mentioned her black Mongol eyes. A son followed three years later but the marriage had apparently deteriorated so badly by then that this son may not have belonged to Robineau-Duclos.

The facts here are supplied by a local Juge de Paix who made a report to the Procureur Impérial in 1865. Sido could apparently no longer tolerate her husband and he had been relegated to a solitary bedroom. There were rumours that Sido had taken at least one lover, if not two. The more assiduous of her admirers was a newcomer to the district. 'There is hardly any doubt,' wrote the Juge de Paix, 'about her relations with Monsieur Colette, and there is nobody who is not convinced that Madame Robineau's second child is not the work of Monsieur Colette.'

If this report is accurate, even the solicitous Sido had given up any attempt to reform her husband and apparently she did not even look after him during his last illness. He 'died from a sudden attack of apoplexy, he died at night in a remote bedroom where, although he was ill and was succumbing to the excesses of his drunkenness, his wife would leave him alone ... his wife who, at the start of her marriage, had tried to combat his passion, abandoned him to it completely after her liaison with Monsieur Colette.'

The newcomer who conquered Sido had come, as she had, a long way to the Puisaye. The son of a naval captain, Jules-Joseph Colette was born outside Toulon, at Le Mourillon, in 1829. In 1950 Colette asked Emmanuel Davin, a French journalist, to find out what he could about her father's family, and he discovered that Jules-Joseph's parents had moved from No. 65 – which still stands – to a smaller house in the same boulevard in 1862. The boulevard has been renamed Eugène Pelletan.

There has also been speculation about the origin of the name Colette, which may possibly derive from Saint Colette Boilet who was born at Corbie in Picardy in 1380. The name may have originated in Provence for in the old Provençal language the word *couleto* exists, meaning a kind of strainer or else a small hill, the word being obviously related to the French *colline*. This seems the most likely origin since there used to be in Toulon itself a path leading to a small hill on which a fort once stood. The path was called 'le Chemin de la Colette'. In a much-quoted passage from *La Maison de Claudine* Captain Colette's wife, Sido, laughs at the 'Italian', the 'knife-man', she had married. Sido's granddaughter, Colette de Jouvenel, has also referred to the Italian origins of the family.

Before reaching the Puisaye Jules-Joseph Colette had known a life of action. He joined, not the navy, as his father and grandfather had done, but the army, graduating from the famous military academy of Saint-Cyr when he was twenty-three as a sub-lieutenant. He was posted at his own request to an élite force, one of the new regiments of Zouaves which had just been formed. After a short time in Algeria he found himself in the

Crimea in 1854 and was wounded at the battle of Alma. By the
end of the following year he had already been promoted to
lieutenant and then captain. In 1859 when France under
Napoleon III allied itself with Sardinia to expel the Austrians
from Italy Captain Colette was wounded at the battle of
Melegnano, or Marignan as it is called in France. He was remembered by his colleagues for his courage and his ability to tell jokes
even when suffering great pain. His right leg was amputated
and he was invalided out of the army. He was made a Chevalier
of the Légion d'honneur and then in 1860 appointed by the
Ministry of Finance to the post of tax-collector in that remote
village in the Yonne, Saint-Sauveur-en-Puisaye.

His daughter regretted later that she had in one sense known
her father so little, but it is clear from *La Maison de Claudine*
and *Les Heures longues* that she understood his state of mind
very well. Saint-Sauveur is a village delightful to see, but possibly
uninteresting to live in. After the excitements of the Crimea and
Italy life for the Captain seemed to be over by the time he was
thirty. His work as a tax-collector was in no way absorbing and
he returned to politics, the passion of his youth, a passion which
has so often preoccupied retired military men. As life went on
he became more deeply but always unsuccessfully involved in
local elections, but in the meantime he fell in love.

This time there was no arranged marriage. The law did not
allow a widow to re-marry until nine months after her husband's
death and it did not allow her to re-marry during the daytime.
Sido then married Captain Colette exactly nine months after
Robineau-Duclos' death and at eight-thirty in the evening, in
Saint-Sauveur. Afterwards, according to the late Roger Senhouse
in his preface to the translation of *La Maison de Claudine*, the
Captain 'took her and her two children to live in the village', but
this was hardly the case. The Captain had married a rich widow
and the family lived in the house she owned, a solid house where
the railings flanking the stone steps were twisted into two initials

27

– RD, Robineau-Duclos. This wrought-iron monogram is still there today.

A new life began for Sido and the Captain, and the next few years were surely the happiest that either of them knew. The house was comparatively large, with a carriage entrance at the side leading into a yard surrounded with barns and outbuildings. At the other side of the house, completely concealed from the road by a high wall, was the garden : the relatively small garden which was to become one of the best-known in French literature and initiate a whole chain of research by scholars and others based on the theme of 'Colette and the earthly paradise'.

Sido's third child, Léopold, was born here soon after and her fourth and last, Sidonie-Gabrielle, on 28th January, 1873. In one of the last books she wrote this daughter later recounted what she had been told about her birth 'in a room which no one could ever sufficiently heat'. She wrote that she had been born after forty-eight hours of labour. 'The servants round [my mother] lost their heads and forgot to make up the fire in the hearth.' Since the baby girl was born 'blue and silent nobody thought it necessary to pay any attention to me'. Although born 'half-choked' she showed 'a personal desire to live'. The room, she remembered, was lacking in comfort and contained an odd assortment of furniture : twin beds with curtains of flowered cotton, a strange shoe-cupboard used as a seat and a three-section wardrobe with mirror, 'in rosewood lined with satin-like citron-wood', which she always found, during the fifteen years she knew this unchanging room, 'too handsome, and out of place. . . .'

A house which earns the name of home is invariably full of such odd contrasts and even when things are out of place it would not occur to anyone to remove or re-arrange them. Home does not change. At Saint-Sauveur, during Colette's childhood, nothing changed, and when later she wrote about it she made no changes herself, apart from those which had been imposed by her unconscious mind and were therefore outside her control. The house and the garden were inseparable from the personality of Sido and ever since the mid-twenties, when *La Maison de Claudine* and *Sido* were published, this threefold image has gradually become established as the 'still centre' of Colette's work, the clue to her personality and the part of her writing most likely to endure as 'classic'. Since most people's lives are conditioned by what they remember of childhood and home, these books had all the ingredients which destined them to a long life among readers of different types in different countries. Knowledge of Colette's work has grown along with her reputation and it is now no longer necessary to quote in detail the descriptions of daily existence in 'Claudine's house', although few biographers have ever been able to resist doing so, especially since they could not hope to improve on Colette's own evocation of her childhood.

It is possible now to see how the threefold image dominated Colette's work. The garden at the Saint-Sauveur house, where Colette obviously learnt, in her mother's company, to live surrounded with flowers, trees and pets, is invisible from the road; all that can be seen of it are the trees and the iron fence on top of the wall which is still partly destroyed every year by the irrepressible wistaria which Colette herself described. Its flowers provide souvenirs for pilgrims to the village and are even taken back to the United States by visiting admirers. The walls were always high, and other houses in the village present the same aspect. This garden was a large part of Colette's world when she was a child : it was a hidden, enclosed world. Obviously the family went out and the children roamed round the woods and fields and played by the ivy-covered 'Saracen tower' which now figures in the 'Pays de Colette' postmark applied to letters by the village post office. But the garden, which for Colette represented an earthly paradise, helped to separate the family from reality. Perhaps this was one of the reasons why the children, with the exception of Achille Robineau-Duclos, never found it simple to come to terms with ordinary life. Neither Sido nor the Captain had known easy happiness when they were younger. Unconsciously, during the first ten years or so of their marriage, when they had few worries, they created for themselves and their children a family life that was, in Colette's version of it, almost too good to be true, and possibly too inward-looking. It was an idyllic childhood, watched over by gently unconventional parents, but the idyll was not unbroken. The sinister presence of Jules Robineau-Duclos was not limited to the initials on the iron railing. Perhaps the shadow of this solitary alcoholic hung over his daughter Juliette whose behaviour seems to indicate a near-autistic nature. She rarely looked up from her book and old photographs show a frightening expression in those strange Mongol eyes. The village was surprised when Juliette married. The marriage led to estrangement from her family and eventually she hanged herself. Sido would complain that she was always exhausted after brushing her eldest daughter's too-long hair and she admitted that she had never understood her.

Achille Robineau-Duclos became a hard-working country doctor, who married and had two daughters. His life was normal, uneventful and no doubt happy but his younger brother Léopold was not so fortunate. It is clear from *Sido* and *L'Etoile Vesper* that he never grew up; when he was middle-aged his mother still hoped he would keep up his piano practice; Colette referred to him as *le vieux sylphe* and recounted that he would visit her sometimes in the Palais-Royal and talk about Saint-Sauveur. Obviously he had never left it and lived only in the past, complaining that meddling strangers had actually dared to oil the hinges of a gate that had always creaked. Change was wrong, he could not bear it.

The 'Sido' whom Colette immortalized has become a splendid character in literature, but Madame Jules Colette does not seem to have been very skilled in bringing up a family—she may have taught them a good deal about gardening, about trees, flowers, animals, she encouraged them to read and play the piano, and she endowed Colette especially, Achille to some extent, with natural curiosity. But she did not teach them about reality. 'A happy childhood,' wrote her daughter in 1924, 'is a bad preparation for human contacts.'

Sido and her husband had a passion for reading; they had time, servants and few distractions, but reading does not often tell people how to live. Sido read the classics and found it strange that children took so long to enjoy 'good writers' such as Saint-Simon. According to her daughter, she also read Corneille in church, hiding the book inside her missal. Juliette read the classics and magazine serials of all types, she read so much that she hardly ate and 'seemed surprised to meet us about the house'. Colette herself read everything. Some Zola was forbidden but she stole one of the books in question and was so upset by a description of childbirth that she fainted. Captain Colette, like his wife, read periodicals such as *La Revue des Deux Mondes* and newspapers of radical views, for he never gave up his interest in politics.

When other people are mentioned in Colette's recollections of her early life they are usually objects of slight curiosity, like the pretty Nana Bouilloux waiting in vain for a splendid Parisian admirer who never arrived, or Madame Bruneau, to whom Captain Colette made 'scandalous suggestions'. The Curé had no success, for in any case Sido was a free-thinker who only made concessions to church-going when it was necessary to keep the peace and when she thought that her family should be given the chance of seeing what religion was all about.

Sido was a complex person, or at least her daughter saw her as such for she allowed her children to go to the church for catechism. She also took her dog to Mass and said that there was no reason why he should not bark during the elevation – it was his duty as a dog. She was ready to employ pregnant country girls as servants when no one else would give them a home but laughed at her daughter when she wanted to go to servants' weddings.

Other people may have been considered tiresome but they could not always be avoided, especially when the young Gabrielle went to school. Her mother had become so possessive of her youngest child that she refused to send her away to school. It is only a few moments' walk from the house to the school building which has scarcely changed since Colette worked for her *brevet élémentaire* there. It is not surprising that schooldays are passed over in her autobiographical books, for Colette is evidently re-collecting them in *Claudine à l'Ecole*. While one is able to distin-guish the fictional aspects from those which relate more or less directly to life in Saint-Sauveur, it is difficult to see much resem-blance between Mademoiselle Sergent and Mademoiselle Olympe Terrain, the highly efficient young woman who taught Colette. Photographs of her taken during the 1880s show her to be small, compact and authoritative, not unattractive; she was not without admirers, accepted the advances of the drunken Docteur Merlou after the ball later described in the novel and was caught in a compromising situation by her mother. (This doctor was Captain Colette's political rival.) She never married although she acquired a son. She had an excellent memory and as late as 1930 she said of her former pupil Sidonie-Gabrielle Colette that 'in French composition, whatever the subject to be dealt with, she would bring to it a rare precision, the right word, colourful expression and the pleasant surprise of the unexpected'. On another occa-sion she is said to have referred not too kindly to Colette's 'in-gratitude', but fortunately she and her former pupil were later reconciled. It seems likely that her teaching helped Colette to go a little further than the reading she did at home under her parents' eyes and it is a pity that we know of her only through the *Claudine* books. Yet the circumstances under which those books were written did not encourage their author to re-use the material in any other way.

Reading was not the only occupation of the Colette family, although they seem to have enjoyed it more than any other. Enjoyment was the most important aspect : nobody read because they felt they had to do so, even if Juliette Robineau-Duclos may have done so to protect herself against the world. There was no 'literary' society in the Puisaye. Sido, sometimes accompanied by her daughter, made a trip to Auxerre, the *chef-lieu*, every month or so, and enjoyed revisiting her native Paris; sometimes travelling actors would come to the village, but their performances seemed depressing even to the young Gabrielle Colette. The village of Saint-Sauveur is so remote that even today only rare country coaches link it to Auxerre. One of the villages they pass through is Toucy where Pierre Larousse, the great lexicographer, was born in 1817. The critic Pierre Trahard whose study of Colette is a valuable contribution to the understanding of her personality and work, makes much of the fact that Rétif de la Bretonne was born at Sacy in the Puisaye, only about fifteen miles from Saint-Sauveur. Trahard points out that Rétif and Colette shared the same heritage, for the Puisaye, along with the Avallonais, had inherited neither 'the Jansenist austerity of the Auxerrois' nor 'the Catholic austerity of ... Orléans'. The people are 'knowing, lively, restless, very close to natural instincts'. He found that the area was not remarkable for virtue or modesty. 'Precocious boys, forward girls, liberal with certain gifts, ready too soon for certain "pleasures", old people full of sudden reawakenings ... nothing which should cause surprise or indignation.'

It is unlikely that the bookshelves in Sido's house contained *Le Paysan perverti* or *Monsieur Nicolas* for Rétif would not have found much favour, even with the liberal-minded Sido. Captain Colette's reading included scientific journals and the political news that was essential to him. His attempts to establish himself on the political scene provided entertainment for his daughter, his 'agent' for a time. He also wrote speeches and proclamations. In

33

local politics he was a failure and as he gave up his ambitions in this sphere he hoped for success in another, that of his own writing. He composed poems, which were bad, although treasured by his daughter and published with her permission as she approached old age. He spent a great amount of time in the upstairs room which was known as the library, and the family assumed that he was writing, filling the large volumes which stood, carefully bound, on the shelves. But after his death it was discovered that the endless sheets of cream-laid paper contained not a single word. The Captain had been unable to face the reality of writing.

Only much later in life did Colette realize how little she had known her father. During her middle age she seems to have been obsessed with Sido and it is evident that this ever-present mother dominated the youngest child whom in her own way she loved so much. Throughout *La Maison de Claudine* and *Sido*, there are revealing glimpses of the mother-daughter relationship. The child was not to go to a boarding-school; was she safe, so far from her mother, when she moved into her sister's bedroom after Juliette's marriage? She was much prettier when she looked stupid, it was a pity it happened so rarely; she had acquired the habit of expressing far more than the occasion warranted, one of Sido's own failings. Sido seems to have relished any sign showing that her daughter had inherited something of her own nature, and it seems odd that she called her 'Minet-chéri', a name much more appropriate for a cat. She was jealous of her daughter's affection for Madame Saint-Alban, a neighbour in whom the young Colette appreciated everything that was different from Sido. She put an end to the father-and-daughter electioneering expeditions when she discovered the child had joined in the wine-drinking with local councils.

Sido's domination of the family was the most dangerous of all because it was insidious, not authoritarian. No wonder the children found other people difficult to deal with as they grew up; no wonder Captain Colette withdrew into his fantasy world of non-existent books. Everything about Sido, as this enhanced character reaches us through her daughter's skilful remembrance of things past, seems wholesome, intelligent, unconventional, warm; but this did not stop her from unconsciously making life difficult for those about her. She organized other people's emotions rather as she drew up shopping lists. It seems a pity that she had no interest in business and financial affairs, because she might have dealt with them briskly, but at this period in France women had few rights and little encouragement even to manage their own property. Sido left all this to her husband.

This aspect of reality interested him just as little as any other. He was utterly bored with his work as a tax-collector and had once faced possible dismissal for inefficiency; he preferred an easy life of reading and would-be writing, while the famous old photograph that shows him playing dominoes with his adored Sido seems to perpetuate the life he obviously preferred. He was given to singing cheerful songs when he felt depressed, and when his daughter was about twelve he must have begun to sing them more frequently. In spite of Sido's splendid dowry from the estate of her first husband the family suddenly found they had no money. Captain Colette had apparently so mismanaged his wife's property that he had achieved only confusion and failed to bring in the revenues it should have yielded. Incredibly enough he was even forced to borrow money from the tenant farmers who did not hesitate to charge him high rates of interest. When Juliette married it had been necessary to scrutinize the family accounts before the usual settlement could be made, and the findings had been alarming. Before long several of the farms were sold and the Captain sold his own house near Toulon. The situation deteriorated rapidly and when Colette was sixteen came the final blow : the house, with its magical garden and all its memories, was sold by order of the court and the family's personal belongings put outside in the street.

There was only one place where the family could go. Achille Robineau-Duclos, the doctor, lived not far away at Châtillon-sur-Loing, now Châtillon-Coligny. He was prepared to harbour his mother, stepfather and their two children, Léo and Gabrielle. The Colette household left the village, and Colette herself never forgot that day.

# 2

## *Interlude in Châtillon-sur-Loing*

Slightly larger, slightly more urban that Saint-Sauveur, the little *bourg* where Doctor Robineau-Duclos harboured his family in 1889 is now known as Châtillon-Coligny, having taken the name of the famous sixteenth-century Admiral whose family had owned and rebuilt the old château here. The Doctor lived at the house which is now number 3, rue de l'Eglise, a house which would not have provided a great deal of room for his dispossessed parents and their two younger children. It was tall and narrow, with stone steps in front and no garden, only a little *cour intérieure*. The famous photograph of the family seated on the steps shows that Sido's face is thinner than in earlier pictures but the Captain, as usual, looks cheerful and unabashed. Although Colette rarely smiled at the camera, she looks cheerful too, the rounded schoolgirl's face is developing the triangular outline that was to characterize it for most of her life.

Colette had left school and was to spend four years here. She has left us few details describing how she spent her time, although some of the incidents described in *La Maison de Claudine* may be partly based on her memories of this period. It was here apparently that Captain Colette used an upstairs room as his 'library' and continued his pretence at writing. Of Sido's activities, now that she was bereft of her garden, we are told little. Colette herself was happy in the company of her elder brother, who was apparently her favourite, and especially in the intriguing short piece entitled *Le Sieur Binard* she tells us a good deal about him, how hard he worked, how handsome he was, so attractive that an eighteen-year-old peasant girl pretended she was pregnant in order to attract his attention. The doctor responded to her advances: 'usually my brother would go to join her in her field. She would watch out for him at a distance, put down her hoe and bend down under the branches to enter a young fir plantation. From these almost silent encounters a very beautiful child was born. And I admit I would be glad to see, even now [this was 1937], what he looks like.' Sido found the baby so delightful that she could easily have taken him away: he had curly hair and a mouth she found irresistible.

Achille Robineau-Duclos had inherited from Sido the curiosity about the natural world that was shared by his younger half-sister, and together they would pick bluebells or mushrooms, tease snakes and collect butterfly chrysalids. Colette enjoyed his company and admired him so much that she decided she wanted to be a doctor. She often helped him dress wounds and in the afternoon she would accompany him on his rounds, holding the reins while he visited his patients in their isolated farmhouses and cottages. One of his responsibilities was a monthly visit to the babies in the area and Colette remembered vividly that he would return deeply upset by what he saw, for many small children were abandoned all day in the empty houses while the parents were out working in the fields. Her much-loved brother worked hard at his country practice for more than twenty-five years, and his only distraction was music, another taste which she and her other brother Léo shared.

The family then remained together, except the married Juliette who had stayed behind in the Puisaye area and in any case no longer spoke to them, even to her mother. Life could have drifted on uneventfully for many more years had it not been for the Captain's intense, if uncreative interest in the literary-scientific magazines which he received regularly from Paris and the contact he had faithfully maintained with his former colleagues from the early years spent at Saint-Cyr and in the military campaigns that followed. The most outstanding of these colleagues was Albert Gauthier-Villars, whose family came from the Jura. After showing brilliant academic promise at the Ecole Polytechnique he became an inspector of telegraphy at the age of twenty-five, fought with the French expeditionary force in the Crimean campaign and was present at the siege of Sebastopol. In 1859 he organized telegraphic communication for the French army fighting the Austrians in Italy, where he met Captain Colette. His work at Novara caused him to be made Chevalier de la Légion d'honneur at thirty. In 1864 he took over the old scientific publishing firm of Bachelier which numbered Sadi Carnot among its famous authors. Albert Gauthier-Villars streamlined the entire organization, acquired the publication rights for governmental and leading scientific publications and achieved such improvements in type-face design for the printing of algebraic formulae that the *caractère Gauthier-Villars* still exists in typefounders' catalogues. The firm prospered and soon acquired the rights for publishing the work of Auguste Comte, Camille Flammarion, Pasteur and Henri Poincaré. Its offices still stand on the Quai des Grands-Augustins, in Paris.

In 1888 Albert Gauthier-Villars' two sons, Henri and Albert joined the firm. Henri seemed destined for a brilliant future; he had won a poetry prize at the Collège Stanislas and published sonnets when he was nineteen. A few years later came essays on such different subjects as the Parnassian poets and Mark Twain, a far cry from the commercial side of the Gauthier-Villars publishing house for which his father made him responsible. He worked there for a time and his name appears on at least two of the firm's publications, *Traité de Ferrotypie* and *Compendium sur la Photographie des Objets Colorés*. But Henri did not relish the prospect of a lifetime spent in continuing his father's work.

His interests were wide, among them oriental languages, cunei-
form writing and music. After two or three years in the family
firm he broke away into literary work and journalism where he
felt he could express himself more satisfactorily.

Meanwhile, Captain Colette had kept up a correspondence
with Albert Gauthier-Villars. They shared an interest in all
aspects of science, and were both members of the Société de
Géographie. It was natural, then, that his friend's son, Henri,
should visit him. Perhaps it was just as natural for Henri to fall
in love with the Captain's daughter.

In 1891 Henri Gauthier-Villars was thirty-two, somewhat bald,
ot handsome but witty and entertaining. He was known in
Paris as 'Willy', his friends included writers such as Verlaine,
Moréas, Henri de Régnier and Anatole France, but he probably
realized he could never equal them. After his reaction against
the scientific solidity of his father's world, he began to prefer the
light touch and the wide range. As the firm of Gauthier-Villars
went on to publish Bertrand Russell, Marie Curie and Einstein,
'Willy' wrote – or was assumed to have written – light novels
which tried to shock, while he also became the knowledgeable
but often cynical music critic who knew his subject well but liked
to have his signature, his photograph, his caricature everywhere.
Scientific discovery interested him no longer, he preferred new
authors, new playwrights, new composers. Most of all he wanted
to discover and assert himself but in so doing he went to endless
lengths to hide himself, from others certainly, from himself,
possibly. Perhaps he was to some extent afraid of being himself,
perhaps he was even afraid there was no 'self'. He wanted to be
everywhere at once and write every book; he could only achieve
a semblance of this by using many pseudonyms and employing
many impoverished scribblers to ghost the books for him. He
was a strange man, his strangeness due partly to a reaction against
his family and partly to the artificial atmosphere of the times.

The family in Châtillon-sur-Loing saw an urbane, not-so-young man who talked entertainingly of Paris and Bayreuth. His family had a country house in the Jura, all seemed highly respectable.

The Colettes had no money, their daughter would have no dowry; Willy was not rich but he was richer than they were, and even if he had left the family firm, there could be no doubt that his background was comfortable. Some emotional biographers have believed that the young Gabrielle was 'sold', as Sido had been 'sold' to Jules Robineau-Duclos in order to ease a melodramatic family situation. It is impossible and more or less irrelevant to make any judgement on this question now. Many girls in the French provinces made loveless marriages because in the 1890s, and later, they often had no choice, but if the Colettes had wanted to arrange a satisfactory conventional marriage for their daughter they would not necessarily have accepted Willy, for he seems to have been the first suitor and he was by no means conventional. He might even have reminded Sido of the bohemian existence she is said to have lived in Belgium with her journalist brothers before her own marriage.

Willy, who had a great appreciation of women and had perhaps tired of the company of actresses and demi-mondaines, found a girl of nineteen who was attractive, intelligent and amusing. He already had a son, but he had never contemplated marriage. Few people have had a good word for Willy and it would be easy to say that he was incapable of falling in love. Everything he did seems to have been done for some calculated purpose, but it is fair to assume that as far as he was capable of loving, he loved Colette when he met her. It is also fair to add that Willy could not afford to stop amusing and surprising the essentially blasé and bored people he knew in Paris. Willy married! And married to a country girl barely out of her teens! Not even the most inventive of his friends could have imagined this.

Colette was to write at great length later in life about her first marriage, but she has had little to say about her feelings at this stage. She was flattered, dazzled by Willy's attentions, and such feelings can easily add up to a conviction of being in love. Her half-sister had married, and if Sido continued ever-present and in her loving unconventional way, this is paradoxically enough the kind of mother from whom it was essential to escape. Sido was gloomy, perhaps because she remembered her own first marriage with revulsion. She had already complained that Juliette had married a 'stranger', and that marriage as an institution was barbarous. Sido had not cared to part with Juliette, although she had admitted that even she did not understand her. She was even more reluctant to part with the young Gabrielle, in whom she had found so much of herself and called by such loving names as 'My Jewel of Pure Gold'. In a moving piece of quasi-fiction, published after her death in *Prisons et paradis* Colette wrote what is probably a fairly accurate and at the same time a sad account of a discussion she had with her mother, just before her marriage.

'So, my poor little pet, you're going to leave me? You're going to go away, and who with?'
'But Mama, with the man I love!'
'I know very well you love him, and that's not the best part of your story. In fact it would be better if you loved him less. And what happens afterwards?'
'Afterwards? Nothing.'
'Nothing. You're far gone. The thing I see most clearly is that you're going to go away with a man, and I don't find that very wonderful, my daughter going away with a man.'
'But Mama, he'll be my husband!'
'That means nothing to me, the fact that he'll be your husband. I've had two husbands, and I'm no better off as a result. . . . A man you don't even know!'

Sido confessed later in letters to her daughter that when she became Madame Robineau-Duclos she knew nothing about marriage, and the admission was surely not restricted to letters. Once at least, when scolding Captain Colette, she had reminded him that he was not even related to her.

'. . . A man you don't even know!'

'Oh, but I do, Mama, I do know him!'

'You don't know him, you little silly, because you love him! You're going to go away, all alone, with a man, and your brothers and I will watch you go, with very long faces. It's disgusting that such things should be allowed!'

'But really, Mama, you're extraordinary. What do you want me to do?'

'What you want to do, naturally. But it's not nice. Everything's so badly arranged. Now look! He tells you he loves you and, since you love him too, there you are in his arms and ready to follow him to the ends of the earth.'

Colette had at least learnt some independence from Sido. She was in love, or had convinced herself she was. But Sido may well have been right when she told her daughter that she did not know the man she was marrying. There was a long engagement but the couple did not see a great deal of each other, even though they traced their initials with a diamond on one of the windows of the house. At moments Colette felt herself weaken, for she was often alone and the fact of being engaged gave her a sense of unreality. 'The infatuation of a girl in love,' she wrote, 'is neither as constant nor as blind as she tries to believe. But her pride keeps her brave and self-contained, even in the moments when she will utter the inevitable, heartfelt cry of awakening and fear. That cry had not risen to my lips, for two long years of engagement had sealed my fate without changing anything in my life.' These memories, in *Noces*, were written many years after the event when Colette had as it were organized her recollections, consciously or unconsciously. Willy may have been in love, but this did not interrupt his almost hysterical activities in the world of journalism and publishing. He did not come to Châtillon-sur-Loing very often, apparently, and his betrothed does not seem to have been invited to Paris. 'After becoming my fiancé the friend of my family came rarely to see us, bringing books, illustrated magazines or sweets, and then left again.' Significantly, added Colette, 'The great event of our engagement for me had been our correspondence, the letters that I received and wrote freely.' Those letters, which probably exist no longer, may have allowed the early development of Colette's style as a writer. She has described how she would give 'literary' advice to her father and has also stated that she had no urge to write when young: but two years of correspondence with an almost-invisible fiancé could have provided a good starting-point for a novelist.

It may have been splendid to have a devoted admirer in Paris, but Colette suffered for it. Whenever Willy visited the family she would walk to the station with him afterwards, returning alone with only her dog as companion. Her two brothers would then make unflattering remarks about Willy's increasing baldness while she pretended not to hear. The practical Achille said that the teasing and the possible hurt were good training for married life. At the same time he would console her by taking her out with him in the carriage on his rounds, as he had always done . . . 'he found me, as he knew he would, already installed there with my book, my snack, my old coat, ready for a long journey . . . prepared to endure the loud screams of women in labour, and to look after the mare, plucking handfuls of green oats or fine hay for her enjoyment – in short, to return to my childhood.'

It is sad perhaps that she should have returned to childhood before she was twenty but it was true that all the best of life had been left behind in Saint-Sauveur. The time came to leave not only childhood but girlhood, Châtillon-sur-Loing and her family. As for Willy, he may have been preoccupied with work but he seems to have been happy, for he wrote to his friend Marcel Schwob, the anglophile writer, saying that he was 'Thinking of marriage and completely stunned by the airy grace of my pretty little Colette.' The engagement was nearly over : 'Within a month I shall have married her. And there it is. And I shan't have a penny. *All right!*' The last remark was in English. Willy spent most of his life worrying about money, but for the moment at least this problem did not delay his wedding plans. On 22nd April, 1893 he sent a telegram from Paris at 7.15 a.m. to the mayor of Châtillon-sur-Loing : *Publiez bans Gauthiers-Villars-Colette. Salutations empressées. Gauthiers-Villars.* The telegram has survived and the copy preserved by Les Amis de Colette en Puisaye at Saint-Sauveur has probably been read by more people than any of Willy's books.

The wedding took place on 15th May and if Colette wrote at length about her married life she wrote only once, in 1944, about the day on which it began. It was, like most events in her life, a drama, or it supplied her at least with the elements for a dramatic piece of writing. 'Mine had been a modest little wedding. No mass, just a simple benediction at four o'clock.' A local timber merchant, his wife and daughter had been her witnesses, Willy had brought two friends from Paris. By the time Colette wrote this account she had had a long experience of journalism, theatre and fiction. The wedding was not only modest, in Colette's memory it was a sad little drama which she presented with ironic artistry. Her parents acted their parts and behaved in character. 'At five o'clock Sido rested for a moment, stiff in her faille dress with jet trimmings. Her face was red as it was each time when she felt unhappy and tried to hide it. My father, in his armchair, read *La Revue Bleue*.' Willy's witnesses and Léo Colette went out to play billiards. In fact, nobody, except Sido, seemed particularly interested. Colette went on to remark that even if the wedding were quiet, 'it was not lacking in the unusual. In the first place all photographers, even amateurs, had been banished. The bride had escaped white satin and the headdress of wax flowers. Sprigged muslin gathered at the neck and at the waist, a broad white ribbon tied on my forehead – *à la Vigée-Lebrun*, said my mother – and my long plait lost in the folds of my long skirt; I can see nothing more to say about me except that I was very nice and rather pale.'

Fortunately one amateur photographer must have concealed his camera at a window for the picture he took still exists. The little procession is on its way through the village square to the church; the bride's face cannot be seen, but the white ribbon flutters in the breeze about her head. She is escorted by her father and leans on his arm. Several couples follow them, none easily identifiable, but at the end is Willy, looking somewhat stern, the sunshine gleaming on his bald head. This was probably the one occasion in his life when he positively refused publicity. It would be touching to imagine that on this day he wanted to forget his Parisian existence and devote himself utterly to his bride. This was not the case however, he had even brought his work with him, for he was convinced he could not afford to interrupt his activities for as much as one day. Colette remembered, or chose to remember, that provincial life did not suit him, but he made an effort in his absent-minded way to be nice to the bride : ' "one can't imagine a place where the post goes at five o'clock, and where wedding breakfasts take place at half-past six. I'm still looking for something for my *Publicité Littéraire* in the old Sully-Prudhomme style. . . . I adore you!" '

The bride could not realize she was leaving her parents, her much-loved brothers and country life. Colette remembered that she chewed a mint leaf, poked at an anthill with a stick, added some dark carnations to the bodice of her dress, and, after champagne, fell asleep. The wedding night was apparently spent at Châtillon. 'Next day a thousand leagues, chasms, discoveries, metamorphoses without remedy separated me from the day before. . . .'

The story of her married life was to be completed in *Mes Apprentissages,* published in 1936. Relationships within the Colette family had been complex enough and the youngest daughter had been emotionally unprepared for marriage. Life was to be a long search for happiness; whether happiness was in any way connected with love was one of the problems that was to preoccupy her most. Sido, disillusioned by marriage and loving her youngest daughter to the point of domination, had not wanted her to acquire a husband and leave her. Yet that daughter was so like her mother in many ways that she may well have wanted to escape from her. The themes of restlessness and escape were to haunt much of her writing. She was not unhappy at home – as far as her brother's house could replace the lost home of Saint-Sauveur – but she was still ready to leave it. Marriage coincided with escape, but her loneliness as a bride was characteristic of the solitude that haunted her throughout a crowded life.

The day after the wedding was no less lonely for Colette than the wedding itself. 'I travelled to Paris in an old railway carriage which rolled along with the noise of a stagecoach, accompanied by three men who were all completely unknown to me, although one of them had just married me.'

It is oddly significant that her account of this first marriage ends not with any memory of her husband but with a picture of her mother. She seems to have been more preoccupied with the complexities of leaving her than with the new life that awaited her in Paris. The three men in the railway carriage went to sleep . . . 'my heart was swollen with pain from a mental impression that remained with me. My mother had stayed up

47

all night and at daybreak was still wearing her splendid dress of black faille and jet. Standing at the blue-and-white tiled stove in the little kitchen, Sido was pensively stirring the morning chocolate, her features, unguarded, betraying a look of terrible sadness.'

# 3

## *The Shadow of the Flat-Brimmed Hat*

The distance between Châtillon-sur-Loing, Châtillon-Coligny today, and Saint-Sauveur, is no more than about seventy-five miles. Later in life Colette was to travel all over France, Switzerland and Belgium, visit Italy, Roumania, Spain, Denmark, North Africa and New York, but no journey was ever as long as the one she made on the first day of her honeymoon. Willy possessed a bachelor apartment, a 'garret', on one of the quais, which in retrospect Colette hated. Every time a bus or lorry passed by it rattled; it was painted in dark green and chocolate brown, full of 'unspeakably sordid cardboard files', piles of yellowing newspapers and obscene German postcards. Willy liked its darkness and cherished its untidiness. Colette was relieved to come down the stairs every morning and walk over the nearest bridge to the little dairy-café where she and her husband drank 'pale mauve chocolate', where there was at least daylight. Fortunately Willy did not intend to settle down here. There seems to have been a short honeymoon in the country and a strange photograph has survived, showing Willy wearing a cap or beret with his apparently docile wife sitting on a rock at his feet. They do not look happy, they seem detached and without expression.

The ménage settled down in an 'almost old house' in the rue Jacob on the Left Bank. The house stood between two courtyards and the apartment, on the third floor, was again dark.

Prosper Mérimée had lived in the house next door, Laurence Sterne had stayed not far away and in the adjoining rue Visconti was the house once occupied by the actress Adrienne Lecouvreur, mistress of the Maréchal de Saxe. The garden there contained the little temple she had built and dedicated to 'L'Amitié'. Later Colette was to know the strange *amis* who were her neighbours, Rémy de Gourmont and his 'Amazon', Natalie Clifford Barney. The rue Jacob apartment had been decorated by an eccentric man who had lived there for fifty years and decorated most available surfaces with 'minute diamond-shaped confetti in many colours' which had been cut out and glued in position, one by one. Colette found that she was young enough to tolerate it, ugly and depressing though it all was. The chimney of the porcelain stove in the dining-room was moulded in the shape of a palm-tree. She dared not go into the bedroom during the daytime because she was frightened of the wardrobe mirror, which was grey and distorted, ugly and mournful. She remembered too that it made her think of that other wardrobe she missed so much, 'the tutelary wardrobe of the ancestral home', the wardrobe from her mother's bedroom, 'of rosewood lined with white thuya, impregnated with provincial order, sprigs of lavender and the dried petals of red roses'. Home was still in Saint-Sauveur, the young Colette found it hard to realize that home for her now was the presence of Willy.

Between her marriage and the publication of *Claudine à l'école* in 1900 lie seven almost undocumented years. In 1894 Jules Renard noted in his *Journal* that Colette had been remarked at the première of a play for her long plait of hair and her loud laugh. She was also remarked, and again her long plait was mentioned, when she opened the Ecole Polytechnique ball with her father-in-law, Albert Gauthier-Villars. Her dress was sea-green with a lace cape, and she did not look well. This was not surprising, for the effort of adjustment she had had to make demanded an almost superhuman strength. Life with Willy was neither leisured nor comfortable. In later books, spread over a period of some forty years, she described something of what happened; her admissions and her reticence allow the reader to judge the situation.

It was some time before she could admit to herself the degree of disillusionment she experienced during her early years in Paris. In *Mes Apprentissages* she wrote, in 1936, that she found it very difficult to accept that the existence of a wife should be so different from that of a young girl; life in Paris was even more different from life in the country than she had imagined. The most saddening aspect of her new life was perhaps the difference between 'happiness – or in any case the illusion of happiness – and its absence, between love and the laborious, exhausting pastime of sex.' If she had experienced emotional and sexual happiness she could possibly have borne the shock of this new life, but without such happiness how could an inexperienced girl have tolerated Willy's frenzied attempts to earn money and keep himself in the news? She also discovered that the brilliant writer, the learned music critic whom she had adored from her provincial village was no writer at all, but merely a clever man who organized other people to write for him. His activities were quite simply sordid, the books he wrote, or rather signed, were third rate and he was preoccupied to an abnormal degree with financial detail. So preoccupied in fact that his wife had no winter coat and he did not enjoy giving her housekeeping money.

No wonder that the young bride felt trapped and any illusions she had possessed about Willy, perhaps about all men, about love and possibly about literature vanished with unusual speed. She realized many years later that 'young girls enjoy the company of mature men but secretly it depresses them. My husband was fifteen years older than I was.' She admired older men and various of Willy's friends 'adopted' her, but she missed the company of women and most of all she missed her mother. The inherent dangers of the family situation during her childhood now overtook her. The father who had somehow never been real to her – she admitted this sadly in later life – had in some way to be replaced. Willy was no father-figure, but in some ways he had had the semblance of one, especially before marriage. His friend Paul Masson, brilliant scholar and eccentric practical joker, became one of her most valued companions. Another of her favourites was the extraordinary Marcel Schwob, who was to initiate her into reading Kipling and other English authors.

To say that she missed Sido is an understatement. She was almost unable to live without her. 'Every day, in order to beguile my ceaseless craving to be with her, to live beside her for ever, I wrote a letter to "Sido".' She admitted that she could not even manage the long hair that was so admired in Paris when she was young. 'I could brush and plait it, but in other ways I was clumsy : I could not dress the long hair that my mother's hands had never pinned into a chignon.' If she felt cold she would unplait it and feel warmer as it enveloped her like a cape. 'At night I plaited it again; and dreamed of snakes when the ends of the braids caught between my toes.' The loneliness of being the young Madame Willy overwhelmed her, and life without the dominating, if loving Sido, could not go on. The saddest aspect of this relationship is that Colette could not bring herself to tell her mother about her unhappiness. The possessive mother who hoped to organize her daughter's life naturally longed for confidences, but such was Colette's nature that she could not possibly tell Sido what was happening to her, she could not bear to admit that Sido's attitude to the marriage had been proved right. The human organism has an infallible method of dealing with such a situation; Colette became ill, partly at least through depression, as far as can be judged from the details of Claudine's illness in *Claudine à Paris*, a book which closely mirrors many aspects of its author's life.

The doctor from Saint-Lazare who treated her scolded her gently because she made no effort to get better : 'Help me a little! I'm trying so hard to cure you and you're not doing anything!' It is sad to read in *Mes Apprentissages* that Colette actually realized she was near death, simply because she had no will to live. 'There is always a moment in the life of young people when death seems just as normal and attractive as life, and I was hesitating'. She was saved however not so much by the doctors as by her mother, who came to Paris to nurse her. Sido made no secret of her feelings about her son-in-law but she saved her daughter.

Colette's mental and physical state before, during and after this long illness – her first and last – take up a good many pages in *Claudine à Paris*, which was written several years later in 1901. It is from the four *Claudine* titles that almost all the details can be filled in to form a clear, if saddening picture of her existence at the time. Her depression and physical collapse were not due entirely to a lack of country air nor to her discovery that Willy, as a writer, did not exist. Soon after realizing that he was not a good husband, not a satisfactory father-figure, she realized that he was ready to be unfaithful to her after only a very short period of marriage.

The value of following Colette's life in some detail is that it reveals clearly her method of working. Many novelists have used fact as a basis for their fiction, but few have used the experiences of their own life to the extent that she did. As her career as a writer developed she wrote 'factual' books such as *La Maison de Claudine* and *Sido* where memory and artistry produced an individual type of writing: 'real' people move in and out of the story until the reader is no longer sure where 'fact' begins and ends. Fortunately Colette recorded one incident in her early married life which shows her state of mind when forced at last to face up to what could be called an 'adult' situation. She treated it as a play, instinctively acting her part with calm dignity. This may have been because Charlotte Kinceler, the young woman concerned, herself had ambitions to become an actress.

Since the Willy entourage included many actresses and music-hall artists, such as the young Polaire and the older famous Spanish dancer la Belle Otéro, Colette had rapidly become used to a type of behaviour which brought drama, even melodrama, into everyday life. After receiving an anonymous letter one day the young Madame Willy found her husband and Charlotte Kinceler 'not in bed but sitting in front of – again! – an account book'. Colette tells this story brilliantly in *Mes Apprentissages*. She realized that if she had spoken or moved her rival would have flown at her – with the scissors she was holding in her hand. 'Was I afraid? No, I wasn't afraid. Tragedy, the hope of disaster, blood, a loud scream – at twenty, if you look into yourself, you can see tragic landscapes every day that are far finer than that.' A remarkable admission in fact of her state of mind at this period. In spite of the trouble-free childhood and the tranquil garden-life of Saint-Sauveur there was a part of Colette's nature that needed drama, and where there was none, she tended to manufacture it, or so it would appear. Sido, who had always been hopeful that her daughter would take after her, wrote to her on at least two occasions saying that she had inherited her 'love of cataclysms'.

The discovery of Willy's unfaithfulness was a 'cataclysm' for his young wife, who may have become quickly if painfully resigned to an existence without love but was not yet ready to be excluded and deceived. Charlotte Kinceler was no doubt only one of the women with whom Willy amused himself, and Colette chose to tell this particular story in detail because she learnt much from her – how to be ruthless, for example – and because Lotte's own story was a dramatic novel in itself. She achieved briefly her ambition to act, occasionally made money as a prostitute, treated rich or famous men badly, opened a herbalist's shop, was suddenly overwhelmed with religion and, at twenty-six, shot herself.

It is not surprising that many of the photographs of Colette during her early years in Paris show her as thin and sad. She described, again in *Mes Apprentissages*, how she learnt to control her disillusionment – her own existence, her husband's behaviour, her nostalgic longing for her home and her mother – something was here for tears. 'But you can do away with tears if you put your mind to it; after I had been through a thorough training, I scarcely ever indulged in them.' Her contemporaries at the time noted her unhappy look and her resignation is preserved in the portrait painted by Jacques-Emile Blanche, now in the Barcelona Art Gallery. The remoteness of her downward glance equals her utter stillness and the distant elegance of her silken ball-dress.

The dress indicates perhaps that marriage to Willy and life in Paris were not entirely without compensations of a sort, although at the time the young Colette hardly appreciated them. During the 1890s most people were more interested in amusement and entertainment than in anything else. France was prosperous, exuberant and tasteless. Decoration and furniture were heavy and bad; women, who had hardly any legal and social rights, were extravagantly worshipped and wore clothes of exaggerated and complicated femininity. The 'elegant wits and grand horizontals', when not organizing their own amusements, were keeping a watchful eye on how other people amused themselves. They have found their way into books and even, through Proust, into literature. Many members of this society, at various levels, wrote books themselves. One of the best known of the *grandes cocottes,* Liane de Pougy, wrote a novel called *L'Insaisissable,* but it is apparently much less interesting than her own life or even her 'sapphic idyll' (which produced another novel) with Natalie Clifford Barney, the wealthy American girl who came to Paris about the turn of the century and lived there until her death in 1972. When the remarkable Liane wrote the *Idylle Saphique* she called her friend 'Miss Flossie', a name used by other novelists, including Colette herself, when writing about Natalie Clifford Barney, who was also known, through her long relationship with Rémy de Gourmont, as the 'Amazon'. It was sometimes difficult to tell where life, literature and legend began and ended, so closely did they merge. The social scene was complex, life was lived according to a set of rules and the whole of Parisian society seemed to be performing some vast and mannered comedy against a luxurious, ugly decor and accompanied by a great deal of music, either loud and brash or sweet, insidious and insipid. The literary scene also was complex, with the cross-currents of realism and symbolism, the contrasts between Zola, Anatole France, Mallarmé, Francis Jammes, Pierre Loti, Courteline, Pierre Louÿs. Journalism was developing fast, magazines such as *Gil Blas* and *La Vie Parisienne* were popular and of some quality, since they often published work by writers and critics of standing, even if many of their contributors are now forgotten.

The great writers who were to dominate the twentieth century were publishing their first books – Gide's *Nourritures Terrestres* dates from 1897 – but so far they had gained hardly any public. The prevailing tone was frivolous and everyone worked so hard in an attempt to amuse themselves and each other that the literary production of the period became artificial and seems remarkably unamusing today. The second-rate was never more triumphant; there was of course a constant demand for novels, especially light novels with an undercurrent of sexual excitement, often homosexual, for the superficial worship of women had made heterosexual love somewhat middle-class and boring. A man like Willy was a natural part of such a scene, consciously seeking notoriety during his lifetime but acquiring immortality only through his wife. He was probably not the only man in Paris who ran a literary factory at this period but he did it so energetically and with such flair that he could hardly fail to be noticed. At the same time he was intelligent – Colette herself said so – and had made his début as a writer by publishing serious studies. Writing about literature as he had done he knew such poets as Henri de Régnier and Hérédia, and also Anatole France, for whom he was apparently secretary for some time. That prolific novelist was elderly now, but his mistress Madame Arman de Cailhavet still gave receptions for him. Willy and Colette were often invited and Colette must certainly have made some impression for it is known, through *Claudine à Paris*, that Madame Arman de Cailhavet came to see her when she was ill. French critics believe that the character in the book named Madame Barmann cannot be anyone else. Colette encountered many literary hostesses and it is possible that Willy had hoped she would become one too, thereby enhancing the fame which he so desperately hoped to achieve. Any such ambitions were quickly dashed however, for Colette was not only uninterested in any social advancement, literary or otherwise, but she seemed almost frightened of meeting people, a state of mind clearly described also in *Claudine à Paris*. All her life she was to detest any behaviour which seemed artificial, hypocritical or calculated : she did not argue about it, she merely took no part in it. Her childhood had conditioned her to a spontaneous, easy-going existence but her family had not been much interested in social life. In a revealing piece entitled *Visite* in the 1922 collection *Le Voyage égoiste* she described what would happen if any unexpected, or even expected visitor rang the front door-bell : the children would immediately disappear.

In Paris however Colette could scarcely avoid meeting people but at first she was reluctant. As 'Claudine' she was to describe how she refused to disguise her country accent and how surprised people often were by her speech and behaviour. Perhaps Colette herself enjoyed crushing the artificially polite Parisians with her earthy provincial humour, which she seemed to have magnified when it suited her, and perhaps also there was an element of self-defence in her conduct. In any case her individuality was so strong that she escaped the contagion of the period. Her social life brought her little pleasure but she learnt a great deal from the people she met and was later to write about them with the vivid detail that results from close and curious observation. Some of them, like the erudite Paul Masson, are unknown today, but others were the most famous men of the modern era, including Proust himself. In *Claudine en ménage* she refers to the 'young and pretty' *garçon de lettres* who attached himself to her at one of 'mother Barmann's' receptions. He had fine eyes but 'a trace of blepharitis'; he compared her to Greek statues; 'he ransacked, for me, his memory and secret museums, quoted so many hermaphrodite masterpieces' that her enjoyment of the 'divine cassoulet' was almost spoilt. He gazed at her with his caressing, long-lashed eyes and compared her reverie to that of the young Narcissus, full of *volupté et amertume*. Claudine told him that he was digressing and that her soul was filled only with red beans and little pieces of smoked bacon. Thunderstruck, he fell silent. It is useless to speculate whether Colette read *Les Plaisirs et les jours* when it was published in 1895 but she later became a devoted admirer of Proust and wrote a memorable portrait of him.

If Willy's interest in literature was usually snobbish and self-seeking, his devotion to serious music showed him in a better light, even though he found it necessary to invent another name for himself, that of Henry Maugis, under which to write most of his music criticism. However, his musical contacts enabled Colette to meet many young men who were to become consistently more famous, including both Debussy and Ravel.

Looking back at this time much later in life, Colette reflected that she had taken all these clever people for granted, while acutely missing intimate friends of her own age. Nevertheless, she learned from them, as she had from Charlotte Kinceler. Understanding of passionate sexual love came to her through Polaire, whose many lovers included Pierre Louÿs, best remembered perhaps for his subtly disturbing novel *Aphrodite*. Willy and Colette were once summoned to help soothe a quarrel between the lovers, and Colette has recorded how shaken she was when she suddenly realized the power of sex. Polaire talked to her about 'young bodies' and told her that she 'couldn't know'. Colette realized with a shock that indeed, after several years of marriage, she did not know. She also realized, when she went with Willy to visit his family in the Jura, that so many aspects of normal life were lost to her, living as she did an artificial existence in the midst of an artificial society. She enjoyed the company of her nephews and nieces and realized only much later that one of the things lacking in her life was perhaps 'a child of my own body'. Willy's son Jacques adored her.

No child came, but fortunately Colette was able to make some good friends, most of them writers, for she rarely had the chance of meeting anyone who did not write or aspire to write. One of the best of these friends was Marcel Schwob, who is not internationally known now except to a few devotees. He was a leading anglophile, friend and translator of George Meredith, friend also of Arnold Bennett, understanding admirer of Oscar Wilde, translator of Defoe, also of Kipling and many other English writers whom he would visit in England. He admired Robert Louis Stevenson so much that he went on a pilgrimage to Samoa in his honour, despite bad health. He was something of an eccentric and it was to him that Jarry dedicated *Ubu Roi*; he directed a literary supplement for the newspaper *L'Echo de Paris*, employed a Chinese servant, eventually possessed a motor-car and kept a menagerie in his flat which included a squirrel, a grass-snake and a Japanese dog presented to him by Robert de Montesquiou. The same dog, when nobody was looking, ate Anatole France's kid boots. Schwob prided himself on his capacity for sensing a person's true worth, claiming that he possessed a special gift, unconnected with intelligence. He was quickly drawn to Colette, and some of the earliest surviving letters she wrote after leaving home are addressed to Schwob. They are constantly lively, sometimes silly in an affectionate way and full of details about her life at the time. She cried after reading *Le Livre de Monelle* and Willy had to comfort her and put her to sleep beside him in order to calm her. When she first saw the sea with Willy and Paul Masson the description of their adventures might have been given by Claudine herself. She enjoyed Schwob's own books and translations – especially *Moll Flanders* – and was proud that he wrote about Burke and Hare for she had been the first one to whom he had told the story.

She was also particularly grateful for the company of Marguerite Moreno, the young actress whom Schwob married (in London) in 1900. Moreno was to become probably the best-known French actress of the twentieth century. She and Colette remained friends for life. One of her early letters to Colette gives a picture of how Willy and his wife lived in the 'almost old house' in the rue Jacob, where there 'was a dreary courtyard, a huge cold staircase and a kitchen on the landing, opposite the door of your flat.

'Marcel Schwob took me to see you. He was fond of you, and he already knew what you would do later and he called you Loleth. We came in and I saw you. You were reading. Your endless plait was round you like a snake and you had turned your face towards me, which has not changed except to take on all the beauty of what you have stolen from life. At that moment life refused you so much!'

The two young women had met for the first time during a luncheon given by Catulle Mendès, the poet and critic, at the time when Moreno had been his mistress.

Many years later, in *Le Pur et l'impur*, Colette described herself as living in 'a strange state of disguised relegation and unhappiness'. She referred to herself as 'still very provincial' and physically unsociable to the extent of 'fleeing certain hand-shakes and certain hand-kissings'. She realized that she was 'equally upset at staying alone and forgotten in the apartment which saddened me and at finding myself obliged to go out'. Certainly her state of mind during her early years in Paris was complex enough to haunt her all her life. Even in 1944, when she was just over seventy, she remembered, in writing *Trois ... Six ... Neuf* how she felt, remarking that she did nothing except wait. She waited for her husband's arrivals and departures and waited unconsciously no doubt for something to happen, something she could enjoy. If literary parties did not amuse her she at least enjoyed going to theatres and concerts. These outings were by no means pure entertainment or relaxation, for Willy, omniscient and ever-present, was professionally involved. One of the best things to be said of Willy is that he knew a great deal about music and whatever one's own feelings about Wagner and the 'new' music of the time, he was prepared to accept any amount of unpopularity in his fervently aggressive support of the avant-garde. He went regularly to Bayreuth, usually taking his wife with him, and wrote trenchantly, but unfortunately with much cynicism, about music, in various periodicals. The character of 'Maugis', his pseudonym, almost became a living person and was later to appear not only in books by Colette but also by Willy and even other people. Willy's activities as a music critic brought him considerable notoriety and even led him to have a fight with the composer Erik Satie during a Beethoven concert, not about Beethoven but about Willy's attitude to Satie. Willy tried to laugh things off, Satie was angry and attacked Willy with his bare fists, unsuccessfully. Willy hit back with his cane and it was Satie who was escorted to the police station.

The many concerts and theatres occupied Colette's mind and they probably allowed her the first opportunity to form critical judgements, perhaps even to write them. Willy wrote (or at least signed) a column known as *Les Lettres de l'Ouvreuse* for the paper *L'Echo de Paris* and Colette was thought to be at least half responsible for the articles, together with two writers on music, Alfred Ernest and Emile Vuillermoz, although in *Mes*

*Apprentissages* she only speaks of her exhaustion while reading the proofs late at night in the newspaper office.

Despite the days, even years, of 'waiting', therefore, spent lying on her divan, reading and playing with her cat, Colette was gradually drawn into the wings at least of Willy's curious existence. The only young people she came to know really well were the young 'secretaries' or *nègres* who worked for her husband and through them she met a group of attractive men of her own age, most of them English, homosexual and discreetly well dressed. They treated her well, everyone exchanged jokes and enjoyed themselves, especially of course while Willy was out. Colette herself regretted that Willy's active mind had not found better employment. He would 'organize' whole lists of books by sending telegrams, the ghost-writers would receive synopses, detailed instructions about characters and dialogue, but very little pay. Willy's energy was matched only by his obsession with money and his desire to be a famous writer; unfortunately it was also equalled by what Colette later called his 'agoraphobia' in front of the blank page. She realized that these negative qualities were something more than unpleasant eccentricities : they were symptoms of some deep-rooted mental abnormality due no doubt in part to his family background and exacerbated by the social and economic climate of Paris at the turn of the century.

Colette justified the revelations in *Mes Apprentissages* by stating seriously that she believed him to be 'a born critic' and was convinced that he would have been an excellent newspaper editor. She also admitted that he danced *à perfection* : his life was in fact a dance in which he sometimes took part himself but he usually preferred to direct the other dancers while at the same time organizing the programme notes and the publicity. When he had run the commercial side of his father's firm he cannot have had much to learn for he was a born salesman and publicist. He would do, say, write or at least sign anything which would cause talk about him at dinner parties or in newspapers and magazines. He was not afraid of fighting duels and if he needed help he always knew the 'right' person. When one of the books he signed was banned on the grounds of immorality he was able to call on valuable help – he engaged as defending counsel Paul Boncour, who later became President of the National Assembly while his witnesses included J.-K. Huysmans, author of *A Rebours* and Catulle Mendès, poet, critic and a personal friend.

Willy's search for novelty became so desperate that he tried to achieve a certain exoticism by including foreign names among his pseudonyms – Jim Smiley, or Boris Zichine – which today at least *sound* like pseudonyms. He followed fashion by introducing tangled love affairs between male and/or female homosexuals and 'spicing' the whole thing with lively if silly jokes and deplorable puns. According to Colette he could have written good books but, since he wrote not a single one, it was not easy to denounce him as a bad writer. His entire energy was spent in finding ideas and writers. There were never enough of either and money was apparently always short. What could be 'new' in the late 1890s? Surely everything had been tried. His wife had let him down by refusing to be a hostess. But even if she were not sociable she could talk amusingly enough when she felt happy with a few close friends. While listening to her talk, as Marguerite Moreno had described her one day, Willy had an idea.

# 4

## 'You Are Claudine, and I Am Colette'

The story of how *Claudine à l'Ecole* came to be written and published is in one sense an old story, half known to some of Colette's friends shortly after publication, told brilliantly by her after her husband's death and completed when she wrote the preface to the book at the start of the first volume of her complete works in 1948. Colette never dated letters and considered dates so unimportant that she tended to be vague or inaccurate about them; according to her, however, Willy had ideas of using her as a possible ghost-writer as far back as 1894 or 1895. He was as usual worrying about money.

'You should put some memories about the primary school on paper. Don't be afraid of piquant details, I might perhaps be able to make something of them. . . . Funds are low.'

At the time Colette was still feeling lazy after her long illness, but she began to write about school by using external associations to take herself back there : 'Having found again and bought at a stationer's some exercise books like the ones I had had at school, their ruled pages, their grey lines, red margins, black linen covers bearing a medallion and the ornamented title *Le Calligraphe* brought back to my fingers a kind of itching to do impositions, the passivity of carrying out work which had been ordered. A certain watermark across the ruled paper made me six years younger. On the edge of a desk, with the window behind me, my shoulders crooked and my knees twisted, I wrote with application and indifference. . . .'

No wonder Willy would sometimes refer to his wife as 'this child'. She seems to have started writing as though she were still a schoolgirl herself, and if in fact she began to write as soon after her marriage as she said she did, then the style which came naturally to her would probably have the same ring as the youthful, affectionately silly letters she wrote to Marcel Schwob. She seems to have made a point of writing nicely for schoolmaster Willy, without any 'literary' ambition whatsoever.

'When I had finished I gave my husband a closely written text which respected the margins. He read it through and said :

' "I was wrong, it's no good at all."

'Liberated, I went back to the divan, the cat, the books, the new friends, the life I tried to make enjoyable, that I didn't know to be unhealthy.'

Two years seem to have gone by without any further contribution by Colette to Willy's 'factory', except for her share in *Les Lettres de l'Ouvreuse*, which is not easy to define, although it was once described as being 'more than half', as far as opinions went at least. Colette had become attached to Franche-Comté, where Willy's family lived, and she remembered that she and her husband returned from holiday there one September. She missed the 'bunches of small, sweet grapes', the 'hard yellow peaches with blood-stained violet hearts', but Willy at least came back to Paris full of energy and decided to tidy up his desk, a hideous piece of furniture painted to look like ebony.

To his surprise he found the school exercise books and the pages of tidy handwriting. He thought he had thrown them away. As he glanced at them again he remarked *'c'est gentil'*, 'it's nice'. He decided he had been a bloody fool. 'He collected the notebooks together in a hurry, rushed to pick up his flat-brimmed hat and dashed to a publisher's office. . . . And that is how I became a writer.'

From that moment Colette lost the liberty she had gained earlier when she first handed over the manuscript. She was not allowed to sit back now, she had to 'warm up' the story she had written by adding what Willy called 'an over-affectionate friendship ... (he used another, brief phrase in order to make himself understood)' between Claudine and one of her friends. He also wanted lots of *patios* and *gaminerie*, arch, childish behaviour.

So the story of Claudine was 'warmed up' and on the surviving sheets of manuscript can be seen the evidence of the 'editing' that was to make it into one of the most talked-of books of the twentieth century. Colette added her signature to that of her husband on the contract, enjoyed the silence imposed on her and did not read the preface until it was printed. *Claudine à l'école* was published by Ollendorff in 1900, its cover specially designed by Emilio della Sudda, showing Claudine in a Red Riding Hood cape, wearing 'yellow comic opera sabots' and striped stockings, writing in an exercise book. Colette laughed when she saw this, feeling that nobody would believe Willy's story about a schoolgirl author. Willy seems to have been surprised by his wife's laughter, no doubt because to him the publication of this book was a serious business matter.

*Claudine à l'école* was a sensational success and at least 50,000 copies were sold almost at once, a good number for 1900. None of the serious authors of the time published a major book that year in France : *L'Immoraliste* appeared two years later, and in 1904 Romain Rolland began to publish the *Jean-Christophe* series. It is true that Edmond Rostand published *L'Aiglon*, but it is long forgotten now. In England the scene was dominated by Arnold Bennett, Kipling, Conrad and Shaw, and 1900 saw the publication of *Lord Jim* and *Three Plays for Puritans*. A comparative chronology shows that 1900 produced both *The Interpretation of Dreams* and the short, fascinating study by Bergson, *Le Rire*. In 1900 the majority of readers preferred silly books, and *Claudine* was in fact silly, as Colette was the first to admit. It was successful on a superficial level because it described the archly lesbian behaviour that people liked to read about and described it in a new way, using schoolgirls and their teachers in a country village. Nothing could be further from the brothels and opium-dens which novelists had used so much that they had become merely boring, for too many popular writers had tried to achieve titillating novelty through a mixture of vice and exoticism. Everything about Claudine appeared 'different' and fresh, while at the same time its would-be 'vice' seemed all the more shocking in one way because schoolgirls might have been supposed to be the epitome of innocence. Claudine became so popular that everything was named after her, small manufacturers asked permission to use the name and very soon Paris was buying 'Lotion Claudine', 'Glace Claudine', the 'Chapeau Claudine' and 'Parfum Claudine'.

Today *Claudine à l'école* is not entirely a period piece. There are apparently still readers who accept it at its face value and find it entertaining, but its documentary and psychological value to the student of Colette is nothing short of absorbing. She herself has described how the book was written but she did not and in fact could not describe how in her mid-twenties – if her dating is even roughly correct – she was able to fill those school exercise books with writing so different from the 'imposition' she mentioned. The giggly schoolgirls and their ecstatic 'crushes' are obviously dated, yet there is a buoyancy and at the same time a deep nostalgia about the book that inevitably made it stand out among the earnest or pretentious productions of the symbolists and the tasteless futility of the 1900 entertainment writers. Provided one can ignore the endless exclamation marks, the unfinished sentences, the expletives in *patois*, there are even hints of how Colette was to develop. She wrote only about what she knew and at this stage of her life she could only remember her village and the countryside around it. Her memories were so vivid that even Willy had been amused and sufficiently interested to realize that here was a commercial proposition.

He probably did not understand that vivid memories in Colette's case were caused as much by nostalgia as by her gift for telling amusing stories. Colette longed for her mother's presence, yet at the same time could not feel close enough to her to admit her own unhappiness: it is significant that Claudine has no mother and in fact never knew one, for her mother died when she was born. It was useful for the story that Claudine was something of an orphan and needed to attach herself to an older woman, and for the moment Colette solved the problem of her complex relationship with Sido: there was no mother-figure in any of the following books which were classifiable as 'fiction'. Sido appears in her daughter's writing only after her death, and only in books that were presented as non-fiction, although they could not really be called autobiography. During her twenties Colette could not bear to include in her work any memories of a mother-daughter relationship.

It was infinitely easier for her to transform Saint-Sauveur into 'Montigny' and write of the country life which she missed so much. The nostalgia is unconcealed and is all the stronger because the detail is so vivid, the use of movement and metaphor is such an essential part of the style that Colette could not have written 'dutifully' for very long; she needed to write, for she needed to express her longing for this lost paradise of childhood. There was no love to bind her to the present, she needed, even at this early stage of adult life, to look backwards, for the mingled reality and unreality of memory brought her more happiness than the emptiness and disillusionment of her marriage. In spite of the lesbian yearnings between the schoolgirls and their teachers Claudine seems untouched, the reader somehow feels that she really prefers her 'dear woods' to any of the emotional extravagance described in the book. This is not simply because it is clear today what part Willy played in the book, but because the places seem so much more 'real' than the people, as though both Claudine and Colette genuinely preferred them. In fact the book is full of all the contrasts and intensities which were to set Colette apart from other writers: the sadness, yet richness of nostalgia, sudden, lively humour, a preference for all that is natural but a capacity for studying impartially all that is not – if the opportunity should arise; a talent for describing the essence through the surface, for translating ideas through physical sensation and moving unconcerned through constant action in the unswerving, unconscious search for stillness.

If Colette had felt 'liberated' when her first manuscript had been relegated to a drawer in Willy's desk, that liberation was now over, for Willy was determined to exploit Claudine as far as he could. Later in life Colette was, to use her own word, 'severe' about her first books, but allowed them to be reprinted in the opening volume of her complete works. There were many things she did not like about the books themselves but her strongest criticism was reserved for herself; she felt she had been too compliant, too submissive and easily talked into following her husband's editorial directives. She now found herself to be one of the hardest-worked of the *nègres* and Willy was perpetually telling her to hurry, for as usual he was obsessed with the fear of poverty. According to Colette he would even lock the door of the room in which she wrote. She found that she was beginning to live with Claudine, and, writing later in 1908, she sometimes felt haunted by this character with whom she was too closely identified. Writing had suddenly overtaken life, superficially at least she had surrendered to Willy and in her recollections she admitted later that in common with other women who had been within his entourage she was terrified of him. As reward for her invention and the hours she spent in the locked room she received little more than an occasional pat on the head.

*Claudine à Paris*, published in 1901, may not be a particularly interesting novel but it is a fascinating, if depressing autobiographical document already quoted as background to Colette's early years in Paris. Claudine is brought to Paris because her father, who is writing a vast scholarly work about the snails of the 'Montigny' district, decides he must keep a close eye on his publisher or his great book will never reach the public. Claudine's father is in some ways Colette's father, seen here as actually writing a book instead of merely dreaming about writing. When Colette 'used' him in this way – assuming that she did – she might not have known that his large notebooks were filled with blank pages, but in any case she transformed him into a dedicated, highly specialist if somewhat eccentric author. It has been suggested that the notion of a tome on an obscure subject – and to most people a study of snails in one area of France might be described as obscure – was suggested to Colette by the achievements of a hard-working but unremembered relative of her mother's through her first marriage, Jean-Baptiste Robineau-Desvoidy, who died in 1857. His writings covered subjects of localized interest in addition to more general works published by the Académie des Sciences. He even studied the flies of the canton of Saint-Sauveur, using for 'fly' the obscure word 'myodaire' which according to his biographer, Monsieur Pierre Piétresson de Saint-Aubin (son of Sido's friend Madame de Saint-Aubin), is not in any dictionary.

This second book seems in fact to have included certain memories that had not already gone into the first. When Claudine, her father and their housekeeper move from Montigny to Paris the scene is described with the heroine's usual verve, but the details again are so vivid that the reader feels they are remembered, not invented. 'The physical horror of seeing the furniture moved and the little things I was used to packed up made me as shivery and bad-tempered as a cat in the rain. As I watched them take away my little ink-stained mahogany desk, my narrow boat-like bed in walnut-wood and the old Normandy sideboard that I use as a linen cupboard, I nearly became hysterical.' The cat Fanchette ran away in a panic and, found at last in the coal bunker, was fastened, spitting and swearing into a basket. This seems to be the only occasion on which Colette remembered her first and most crushing house-move, when her family were forced to leave Saint-Sauveur in 1889. *Claudine à Paris* is full of details which are recounted cheerfully enough but scarcely form an essential part of the plot. Sido again seems to be deliberately excluded and the archness of the heroine is even more irritating than in the first book since Claudine has now left school and is beginning to grow up.

The word 'plot' is barely applicable, the book is full of *longueurs*, descriptions of Claudine's long illness, parallel to that of Colette, but written with none of the melancholy overtones of *Mes Apprentissages*; graphic accounts of taking baths in a 'tub', playing with the cat, all in that gloomy apartment so similar to the one in the rue Jacob; and meetings with a former school friend and with her cousin Marcel, a pretty boy, a 'girl in trousers'. Marcel is important in one sense for Claudine naturally meets his father, Renaud, who is a writer. He is also drawn to Claudine. 'He looked at me only for a second, but he's someone who knows how to look.' At the end of the novel he asks Claudine's father for permission to marry his daughter.

One of the most interesting aspects of *Claudine à Paris* is the appearance of the would-be witty music critic, Henri Maugis. Not content with using the name to sign various of his articles on music Willy apparently wanted to continue the shadow-dance of his life into the books he was supposed to be writing. Colette was at pains later to explain that she did not invent this character and could think only that Willy, who liked looking in mirrors, saw himself this way. It is never clear whether Willy suffered from some strange inferiority complex or whether he thought these descriptions of himself were funny : 'still puffed out with honest fury, his porthole-eyes and his congested neck make him look like a somewhat batracian calf'. In any case 'Maugis' was to appear in other books by Colette and also by Willy himself, or to be precise, in other books signed by Willy.

Colette wrote later that *Claudine à Paris* and *Claudine s'en va* gave her the most trouble. Of *Claudine en ménage*, published in 1903, she said not a word. Her only indirect reference to the book later was a comment on the 'hollow' character of Renaud, whom Claudine married, but he after all appears in other books. The first two Claudine titles were 'programmed' by Willy and his contributions, direct or indirect, can easily be distinguished, the result being an obvious loss of unity. But in *Claudine en ménage* there *is* unity. Claudine and Colette come remarkably close to each other here for when Claudine marries the much older Renaud, calling him her *mari-papa*, she seems to feel some of the advantages of marrying someone who, through being older, is kind, considerate and protective. He seems to love Claudine, forgives her childish and sometimes unfeminine behaviour, including her refusal to let him undress her on their wedding-night. He is even jealous of her village, Montigny, for he suspects, rightly, that only the village, and not another man, could take her away from him. Claudine, like Colette, refuses to be a literary hostess and is practically a guest in her own apartment. When she is finally coaxed into half-enjoying social life she remains the amusing country girl with the provincial accent and the talent for intuitive judgements which Colette kept all her life. The scenes at the school in Montigny sound the only false note in the book and were obviously included for those readers who still wanted the piquant details as originally ordered by Willy.

There may be some ineptitude in the handling of Claudine's love affair with the beautiful Rézi, but for the first time Colette seems to be describing adult emotions in an adult way. There is no mistaking the experience behind many unexpected remarks such as, 'You must sit here, close to me, put your head on my knees, don't speak and don't move, for if you move I shall go away . . .' or the scene in which the two women seem to enjoy orgasm while sitting next to each other on a sofa. Could there be greater bitterness than Claudine's realization that her kind husband and her adored Rézi were deceiving her together? Claudine fled to her village, where Colette yearned to go but could not. *Il n'y a pas d'amour heureux* : the pattern was set. For some people loving is more difficult than living and the two cannot always happen simultaneously.

Read without any documentation *Claudine en ménage* is an intriguing book. It is even more tantalizing if one remembers other facts that may be relevant. Colette told the story later of how she developed a 'crush' on a woman who gave her piano lessons for a time. She described her feelings to Jean Lorrain, a writer who happened to be a homosexual. He observed the fascinating teacher. 'Can't you see,' he said, 'she's a man.'

Did Colette write from experience when she described the feeling between Claudine and Rézi, did she write this book as a form of sophisticated joke, to prove that she could produce a story to satisfy popular taste? Did she invent it all? No doubt she used both experience and imagination, as most novelists do, but it would be fair to say that with this book Colette seems to have matured both as a woman and a writer. She may have been sincerely speaking of herself when Claudine mentions the 'pleasant and slow corruption' which she owed to Renaud and wondered how she could protect herself against the 'incurable and seductive frivolity' which carried him away, and her too. Like Willy, Renaud perpetually looked at himself in the mirror, and like Willy, Renaud deceived his wife. Colette may have regarded Renaud as being a 'hollow' character, but it has often been said that he embodies the idealized figure of an older husband. Colette's first individual novel seems to have coincided with her disillusion and what is more important, with her acceptance of it.

*Claudine en ménage* was Colette's third book, and in the

meantime Claudine had appeared on the stage, brilliantly played by the young Polaire, who believed in the part, enjoying it and identifying herself with it. She even told Willy, who had worked hard to organize the dramatization of *Claudine à Paris*, that she *was* Claudine. It is sad to think that Willy even courted further publicity by appearing in public with his 'twins', Colette and Polaire, both dressed in schoolgirl-type clothes, like Claudine herself. Jean Cocteau as a young man saw them sitting together at a rinkside table at the Palais de Glace, and made a sketch of them. Willy, his hands folded over his cane, seems the embodiment of Colette's witty descriptions of him. By this time she had agreed to have her hair cut short and although this might have made her look a little younger it brought a rebuke from someone who by now might have seemed remote: Sido. She wrote to her daughter on more than one occasion that Willy had destroyed what she regarded as her masterpiece, Colette's beautiful long hair. Sido stated that the hair belonged to *her*.

Willy had achieved his ambition for perpetual limelight, or so it appeared, and with his wife standing discreetly by his side, he was written about, photographed, sketched and painted. There were postcards, busts, souvenirs of all kinds and it is hardly surprising that Natalie Clifford Barney noticed that he and Colette 'did not allow themselves the luxury of a private life'. Even Colette, now, after ten years of marriage, was playing a part. She would tease her husband about the women who seemed to be fascinated by him and when other women began to make her offers of 'intimate friendship' she was cool towards them, she wrote that she felt boyish and was used to the company of men. She might have been half aware that she was a professional writer now, even if she still remained anonymous. Willy, as a result of her efforts, had made money and was able to afford a better apartment; she was treated well enough for she was useful – she had a room of her own in which to write, and a lamp with a green shade.

By 1903 Claudine had been in the headlines for four consecutive years and the public had apparently not tired of her; the character of Maugis might have seemed amusing to the contemporary reader, and since there was a half-real Maugis, Willy himself, it was never quite clear who was more important, who had come first and whether nature had imitated art. Colette had acquired such skill as a writer that she was now able to write Maugis-dialogue on her own, without any help from Willy, who would suggest magnanimously that she could 'leave blanks' for him to fill in if she wanted. When she proved that she could manage without him he began to be aware of rivalry, for she reported that his 'bravo' was somewhat chilly. Of the many talents which Colette had already revealed before she was thirty the most notable were curiosity at all levels and a facility for learning both quickly and well. An ability to imitate the silly, offensive chat by Maugis was however a lesser accomplishment than becoming a music critic herself, which Colette succeeded in doing, having no doubt learnt a good deal from her husband and the people she met through him.

Perceptive research by Edward Lockspeiser in London in 1968 regaled students of Colette with the articles that she wrote in 1903 for the magazine *Gil Blas*, called, inevitably, *Claudine au Concert*. Unfortunately they have not been reprinted, possibly because Willy collaborated in their writing. The reviewing work she carried out was shared by no less a musician than Debussy himself, which led to the somewhat unnecessary remark, obviously influenced by Willy, *Mieux vaut Claude que Claudine*, and the new critic even found it wise to assure her readers that she would 'speak very little about music'. Professor Lockspeiser had pointed out that Colette obviously had a detailed knowledge of the Wagnerian orchestra, which at that period was not shared by a great number of people in France, where there was great hostility to Wagner. Colette was not always on the side of avant-garde composers, for she remained unmoved by Richard Strauss. At the same time she – or Willy – wrote one of the very first notices of Mahler outside his own country. Like all the French, she hated Tchaikowsky, referred to Bach as 'a divine sewing-machine' and adored César Franck. She could be as irreverent as Claudine if she wished, comparing Weingartner's arms to the windmills of Don Quixote and finding that Siegfried Wagner looked like 'the back of a bottle'. Her acquaintanceship with Ravel and Debussy was rewarding to her at this period of her life and was to be even more so later, leading to the close and successful collaboration with Ravel in the creation of an opera. Without Willy's teaching she might never have been able to express herself on the semi-technical aspects of music, however much she appreciated it personally, but she had no need of Willy for the addition of those details that made these articles her own. Who else but Colette would have mentioned, before writing about a concert, the lilacs flowering outside the Salle Pleyel?

The articles for *Gil Blas* belong to 1903, when she was apparently still contributing to the *Echo de Paris* column called *Les Lettres de l'Ouvreuse*. At their expense she went to Bayreuth with her husband and in spite of 'some incomparable German voices' she did not enjoy it. However, the background was useful to her for yet another Claudine novel, also published in 1903 and entitled *Claudine s'en va*. Whether it was so titled because she intended it to be the last is not clear, but she wrote later that it gave her a good deal of trouble. The reasons for this are obvious, for the author had outgrown the stage of being an apt pupil, and was unable to resist the need for independence. The new novel was not told in the first person by Claudine but by her friend Annie, while Claudine herself appears in the story as happily married (still to Renaud), somewhat eccentric but mature enough to give Annie much sound advice. The novel does not satisfy as a novel for it is too complex, broken up with not very humorous Maugis humour, mentions of Colette's friends, including 'Miss Flossie' (Natalie Clifford Barney) and Polaire.

1 Colette aged about thirteen.

3  Adèle-Sidonie Colette ('Sido'), Colette's mother.

2  Jules-Joseph Colette (Le Capitaine'), Colette's father.

4 Colette with her parents, her brother Léo (left) and her half-brother Achille (right), at Châtillon-Coligny in about 1891.

5 Colette's birthplace in Saint-Sauveur-en-Puisaye. The inscription (top right) is in her own writing.

6 Colette as a small child, with her brother Léo in the garden of their house at Saint-Sauveur.

7 Colette (left foreground) with the Gauthier-Villars family in Franche-Comté in about 1895. Her husband, Willy, stands on the right.

8 Henri Gauthier-Villars ('Willy'), Colette's first husband.

9 The cover of *Claudine à l'Ecole*, published under Willy's name.

10 Colette and Toby-Chien.

11 Colette soon after her divorce from Willy, on a music-hall tour in Tunis.

12 Colette at Varetz in the Corrèze, with her second husband, Henri de Jouvenel, and their daughter.

13 and 14   Colette in music-hall.

15 Colette soon after her divorce from Henri de Jouvenel in 1924. One of the two cats later became 'La Chatte'.

16 Colette at work.

17 Colette and Maurice Goudeket, her third husband, in their apartment at the Palais-Royal, Paris.

But the sudden detachment of Claudine must surely represent that of Colette. Claudine leaves for the country because in Paris 'women friends are traitors and books deceive'. She is able to go away with Renaud, Annie is forced to go away on her own. Colette's purpose in writing the book was to express the independence, the power she hoped she was finding : the strength to be alone, to be herself. Two books earlier, when Claudine was living in Paris with her father, she had felt the need to lose her schoolgirl independence : 'My liberty oppresses me, my independence overwhelms me; what I've been looking for for months – for longer – was, without my realizing it, a human being. Women who are free are not women.' If Colette herself had felt this once, she felt differently now. Claudine in this last novel seems to represent what outsiders saw of Colette, while Annie in some ways felt what Colette felt. As in most of the books Colette wrote, the mingling of the real and the unreal gives the writing its individual bittersweet flavour while both reader and critic savour the partly-conscious over-dramatic interpretation of biographical fact : 'With sad, passing clairvoyance, I see this second beginning of my life. I shall be the solitary woman traveller who will intrigue hotel dining-rooms for a week. Schoolboys on holiday or arthritics at spas will fall in love with her ... the solitary diner ... the lady in black, or the lady in blue, whose distant melancholy hurts and repulses the curiosity of compatriots whom she meets. ...'

The book was signed 'Willy' like the three which had preceded it. In 1957 a French paperback edition was presented as by 'Willy and Colette'. Claudine had had a long life, and Catulle Mendès' prophecy had come true : 'You wrote the "Claudines", didn't you? ... In – I don't know how long – in twenty years, in thirty years perhaps, people will find out. And then you'll see what it means to a writer to have created a type. You don't realize it now. Oh, it's a big thing! ... But it's a sort of punishment too, a guilt that ... sticks to your skin – a reward that becomes intolerable. . . . You can't get away from it, you've created a type.' Not until 1908 did Colette write about the ghost of Claudine, with whom she would hold imaginary discussions, but by 1903, ten years after her marriage, when she wrote the last book whose title included the name of Claudine, she had established, at least to herself, the fact that she was Colette.

# 5

## *Retreat from Love*

For at least four years Colette had spent several hours a day in a room which was sometimes locked, writing books about a character she had invented, but rarely writing in the way in which she wanted. In each book part of Claudine reflected some aspect of Colette, and obviously the author herself, who had never been allowed to call herself an author, had matured and grown up, irrespective of her partial identification with Claudine, and she had acquired a professional existence of her own. Much later, in 1936, she published her own account of what had happened since she had come to Paris a few months after her twentieth birthday. On the whole there are few reasons for doubting its basic accuracy, in spite of Colette's disregard for details such as dates. Obviously she wrote for publication only what she chose to remember, selecting the facts or the 'slant' which expressed such aspects of the drama as she needed to perpetuate. She did not set out to write her autobiography any more than she had in *La Maison de Claudine*. The arrangement of her material, apparently haphazard, made this clear. Although Colette is at pains to be fair to Willy – he was intelligent, he would have made a good editor, she stated – the reader inevitably remembers the caricature, the description of him as 'convex', or 'like Queen Victoria'. Neither his supporters nor the enemies of Colette, and both have existed, will ever be able to eradicate the memory of the mean, vain Maugis and his over-worked, underpaid, un-acknowledged 'secretaries', *nègres*, ghosts or whatever one chooses to call them. Colette obviously enjoyed recounting the incidents in which she got the better of him, but she did not choose to tell the whole story of their married life.

Without taking sides it must be admitted that these two people were hardly compatible. They had obviously been attracted to each other partly because they were so different, and if such a relationship amused them both for a short time it could not, by its very nature, amuse them for very long. Strangely enough one of the few things they shared at this period of their lives was a tendency to live in a world of unreality, but their divergent natures compelled them to deal with this unreality in different ways and inevitably they moved away from each other. The more Willy wanted fame as a writer and critic the more incapable he became of putting pen to paper; ideas, synopses and publicity gimmicks came to him easily enough but someone else had to cover the sheets of paper with words, or be constantly on hand to take down his dictation. In spite of all he knew about music and musicians he could hardly ever utter a musical opinion in his own natural voice. At the same time he became more and more anxious about money and more given to half-secret, half-publicized liaisons with women who temporarily fascinated him. However, as Willy had given up a respectable career in his father's successful firm in order to play these games with himself and other people, he was presumably reasonably happy with his own neuroses and would have been at a loss without them.

Colette on the other hand was not satisfied with an unreal world. She soon became aware that the life she had thought she wanted was not one that could bring her happiness. She disliked Paris and disliked the bohemian life even more, taking care to say so when she came to write about it. She was often described later as living just such an existence, and when she writes about it in various novels she cannot be said to despise it. She was

attacked for her 'immorality' yet often teased about her 'bourgeois' attitudes and 'respectability'; in fact she was neither conventional nor unconventional, she was outside convention, as
her mother Sido had been. She knew that happiness had been left
behind in the country and realized just as clearly that time is
never regained. She wanted to belong to the real world and
during the years when she began to write she was unconsciously
following a double path : she was escaping from the unsatisfactory reality of her married life and the artificial existence she
was forced to lead while at the same time discovering the reality
of her own self. The rest of her life was to be spent writing and
the artist within her realized that the interplay of reality and unreality, the search for love and the difficulty of accepting it, together formed a unique literary fabric. Its texture and rhythmic
structure, together with its intensity and inherent nostalgia, invariably make the reader aware that the author has found
pleasure in putting the words together, even if that pleasure was
attained after a struggle with every element involved, from
narrative and characterization to details of style.

Pleasure of a superficial kind was of course not entirely lacking
and the young wife who was described as smiling 'in the shadow
of the flat-brimmed hat' was neither ill-treated nor dominated
all the time. In some things she was capable of dominating her
husband and according to one of her letters to Marcel Schwob
Willy allowed himself, when staying in the Jura, to be taken out
cycling before four o'clock in the morning, a far cry from the
cycling to newspaper and publishing offices which was fashionable among their circle in Paris. Colette also had her cat to
amuse her, and later acquired a bulldog, the famous Toby-Chien.
When Willy felt rich enough to move to the rue de Courcelles,
where they lived first at number 93 and then at number 177
Colette acquired a small gymnasium which intrigued visitors to
the house.

But obviously these superficial diversions could never replace the emotional happiness that the young Colette had presumably hoped to find in marriage. Her nature was not one to accept substitutes and although after some years she accepted Willy's mistresses to the extent of teasing him about them she does not seem to have acquired lovers herself. Allegations that she did, and treated them badly, have come from sources so dubious that they merit little attention. Willy was not so much jealous as possessive; he naturally had no objection to his wife's friendships with the young homosexuals who worked for him or with older men like Marcel Schwob. It was typical of Willy that he pretended as a 'joke' that his wife was having a liaison with Schwob, told *her* to tell *him* that they must not advertise the fact, she must leave the carriage a few doors away from Schwob's house. Colette's own letters show that she could accept this sort of thing cheerfully and enjoyed the teasing that seemed such an important part of the friendship – she wanted to roll Schwob up in a giant fly-paper and she referred to him as 'her dearest enemy', a phrase which fore-shadowed the deep-lying love-hate in her nature which was to be reflected later in her own personal relationships and her writing.

She reported that she was not much interested at this stage in the *amitiés particulières* offered to her by women; such friendships were normal in the society of the time and especially in the Willy circle. When he had paraded his twin 'schoolgirls', Colette and Polaire, around Paris, he had apparently tried to spread the obvious story about the two young women – but he was unsuccessful, for Polaire hated what in those days was often called 'unisexuality'. Colette had the opportunity of observing many extraordinary women, notably the slender and fascinating Renée Vivien, the lesbian poet who tried to found a sapphic colony in Lesbos itself. Her poems have been taken seriously by an unexpectedly large number of people, she died young, partly of tuberculosis but mainly of alcoholism, which was all the more insidious because few people ever saw her drinking. She was surprisingly enough an Englishwoman whose real name was Pauline Tarn. One evening when she was at her house Colette realized that the windows were permanently sealed, a depressing proof of the degree to which the poet's life was artificial and futureless. At this stage Colette herself found little difficulty in resisting such an ambiance; she looked at it with some curiosity, did not laugh at it but remained outside. She was to venture inside only later.

In the same circle hovered the observant and omnipresent Natalie Clifford Barney whose aphorisms were eventually to become almost as well known as her lesbian loves and may even give her a lasting if limited reputation. Although essentially concerned with herself, 'Miss Flossie' was one of the few people to have understood something of Colette's personality and behaviour at this complex period of her life. The half-known writer was even more attractive personally than the intriguing old photographs show, she was not merely pretty, her life in Paris had brought out aspects of her character which might have remained secret even to herself if she had remained in the country. On the other hand the country had given her that 'salt' and flavour which Cocteau was to mention so many years later. After ten years of marriage 'she was no longer the slender adolescent with the long plaits . . . but a young woman firmly set on strong legs, the small of her back curving down to rounded buttocks, manners as frank as her speech, but feline silences in her enigmatic triangular face and in those fine blue eyes with their long-slit eyelids a glance which had no need to make itself seductive in order to seduce'.

If women were easily seduced by Colette, her husband found her something of a problem.

As time went on Willy found he had to employ even greater astuteness in 'manipulating' the activities of his wife. He realized that she would not continue, year after year, to write books to his formula and submissively allow him to sign them. The girl who had amused him with her lively anecdotes amused him rather less now, for after the Claudine books and all that followed she was no longer the little country girl he had married. He had always known her to be intelligent but he had not foreseen perhaps that she would hope for independence, since few women did so in the early 1900s, unless they had private means. Colette Willy had become something of an embarrassment and the energy she had acquired by the time she was thirty was not absorbed by looking after pets and exercising in her gymnasium. Although he was pleased when her friends drew her into other activities he still saw himself as her impresario.

It was one thing to live without 'the luxury of a private life', but another for both husband and wife to come to terms individually with the reality of existence. Willy did not easily find the solution to this conjugal impasse. The impresario, having noticed how Colette enjoyed life at Les Monts-Boucons, the house he had bought in the Jura, indicated craftily that she might work faster and better there. This she did, realizing that if Saint-Sauveur was a lost paradise it was possible to find another house and another garden which could in some way replace it. She learnt to live alone there, for Willy's limited visits to his property were intended mainly as 'supervision' from all points of view. If 'Claudine' was to be at least temporarily retired, Colette had still to keep on writing, for Willy insisted that she should, while she herself seems to have accepted by now that she was a writer. Even if the circumstances of the writing were not to her liking, she had been 'trained'. Years afterwards she wrote a message to a friend across a photograph of herself, in schoolgirl clothes, seated on a table next to her dog : 'Claudine and Toby-Chien, two nice creatures who had been taught to "sit up" and hold out their paws.'

At this point the chronology of her writing does not correspond automatically with that of her publications. In 1904 she was apparently working on *La Retraite sentimentale* remembering

in it, with all the more nostalgia, Les Monts-Boucons, for Willy
had decided to sell the house. This book, so important in both
her personal and literary development, was not however published until 1907. In the meantime her relationship with her
husband seems to have become more complex than ever. She
wanted to write not a novel but a short story based on a contemporary news item for which the old fortifications near the
boulevard de Courcelles supplied the background. Willy would
not allow her to publish a 'story', it had to be a novel, he decreed,
and he was still enough of a dictator to win in an argument of
this sort. *Minne* was expanded and published in 1904 and since
a new heroine was something of an investment she had to last
for more than one book, so *Les Egarements de Minne* followed
during the next year. Colette fought hard for permission to sign
these books herself but did not succeed. All she was able to do
was to keep the publication rights for herself. She had invented
a new heroine and seemed fond of the fair-haired girl with
romantic notions who tried unsuccessfully to be depraved, only
to find emotional and sexual happiness with the husband who
had seemed so conventional and boring; a few years later Colette
remodelled the two short novels into one, removing Willy's contribution, but admitted she had been unable to achieve the effect
she had originally wanted. She was in fact as 'severe' later about
the result – entitled *L'Ingénue libertine* in 1909 – as she was
about the Claudine books and since this novel has neither depth
nor documentary interest it might have been preferable to omit it
from the complete works. Its English translator Antonia White
has described it as a 'parody of Colette' and this is perhaps all
that need be said about the book.

Willy's refusal to allow its publication under his wife's name
was all the more frustrating to her because in 1904 he had
seemed more lenient. That year there appeared from the Mercure
de France (where the writer Rachilde and her husband Alfred
Valette, friends of Colette and Willy, took the literary decisions)

85

a little book entitled *Dialogues de bêtes*, signed by Colette Willy; it was enlarged and republished during the following year, prefaced by Francis Jammes, a writer well known for his love of country life and animals. The teasing words *'Pour amuser Willy'* prefaced the book and, although hardly a dedication, revealed the curious state of play at the time. Former friends of Colette's still maintain that this had been the basis of the marriage – she amused him. Perhaps sometimes she still did so and, when she was not afraid of him, or silently angry, he may also have amused her. He encouraged her to go on with the pieces eventually published as *Les Vrilles de la vigne* by writing in the margin that intriguing and now famous remark : *'Continuez donc, charmante petite horreur.'* The use of *vous* is no sign that personal relationships had deteriorated. Willy always addressed her in this way. She maintains in *Mes Apprentissages* that she always addressed him as *tu* – and quotations and at least one surviving letter prove that her memory on this point was right. Willy may have allowed his wife to be an author of a few pieces about animals because he knew very well that such a book would not be a commercial success. It had some literary success however, for it was gracefully done and there was something of a fashion at the time for writing about animals. Nobody, neither Maeterlinck nor Jules Renard had written about them, or, in a sense, through them, as Colette did in these short pieces. Some French critics have maintained that she was influenced by Kipling, to whose work she had been introduced by Marcel Schwob, but there is little direct evidence that this was so. In any case, if the *Dialogues* were regarded as precious by some contemporary critics, others accepted them as an attractive novelty. Francis Jammes seems to have understood what was new about them : 'Madame Colette is a living woman ... who has dared to be natural. Madame Colette Willy has never ceased to be *la femme bourgeoise par excellence.* . . .' If he expressed himself in a somewhat old-fashioned way he realized the remarkable freshness of these subtle yet lightly amusing dialogues. He referred to the author as a poetess who kicked all the muses, with their laurels, buskins and lyres down to the bottom of Montparnasse.

An interesting and indeed reasonable opinion came from someone who was in one sense infinitely more important than any literary critic – from the person who seemed more valuable in Colette's life than anyone else: Sido. 'Yes,' she wrote on 1st April, 1904 (official publication came a year later). 'I've received your delicious little book and I've read it quickly, quickly. Kiki-la-Doucette died from the grief caused by your infidelities in favour of Toby-Chien. Cats are divine creatures and precisely for that reason misunderstood. Only souls above the common run of mortals can really grasp all that is mysterious in the nature of cats; as for their physical beauty, it excels everything. So your book is delightful, but it might possibly not be written for everyone.' There are still readers of Colette who appreciate her writing about animals more than her stories about people; it is possible also to maintain that the animals are not 'merely' animals.

'Colette Willy' had therefore been allowed to exist. Unfortunately however it was obvious now to both Colette and Willy that whatever their professional success their marriage had grown stale and could only deteriorate.

The legend has grown that Colette was so unhappy that she eventually ran away from her husband, but even the evidence of *Mes Apprentissages* proves this to be wrong. She had no thought of running away and had even become attached to her prison; her pride prevented her from going back to her mother and she had no means of earning her own living. Willy took the initiative, encouraged her to think more seriously about appearing in private as a mime, mentioned that it might be possible to appear on the public stage, maybe even to go on tour, adding that there was 'no hurry'.

At this juncture Colette could not hope to be an actress for however amusing she might have been as a story-teller her country accent was no asset in the theatre. Mime was a silent art, demanding maximum expressiveness in face and body. The mime-drama of the period was never far from melodrama and it seemed to offer Colette the opportunity for self-expression that she had only partly found so far in writing. She knew very well that she could not live on what she earned from writing, for even if her friends knew that she had created Claudine, all the contacts with publishers and the general salesmanship had been arranged by Willy. It would have taken a great many animal dialogues – and who would have read them? – to keep her, but apart from her writing, in which Willy had brought her up *aux ateliers*, she had no professional experience. Climbing trees in Saint-Sauveur, she wrote later, had been all very well, but nobody had offered her a job as a squirrel.

Willy, determined now to arrange a separation, embarked on a second period of training. He was perceptive enough to notice his wife's second talent and asked Georges Wague, the well-known actor-mime, to give Colette lessons. Wague found an apt and conscientious pupil, whose liking for gymnastics had kept her in good form. Some sort of career, or at least a capacity for earning some money, seemed possible.

In 1906 Colette found herself in a ground floor apartment in the rue de Villejust. The novel *Claudine s'en va* had been published three years earlier and it was the departure of Annie, more than that of Claudine, which had anticipated that of Colette. The curtain was slow to fall, for she had been unwilling to end this scene and go. It is difficult to forget the drama of those thirteen years, for Colette herself never forgot it. It is equally difficult to see or interpret the facts correctly, but it is very evident that Colette, who had looked for love, had not found it or had been unable to grasp it. As Claudine, she had decided she would live without happiness. Disillusion had been followed, for the first and only time in her life, by hesitation. Willy ended this hesitation, he opted for a realistic solution, but, like the good stage manager he was, he stood for a long time in the wings. Some years before the ménage came to an end Colette had started a new book, *La Retraite sentimentale,* which might be translated as 'Retreat from Love'. It was not published until 1907 and in the meantime Colette had lived through an exhausting and painful period which led her to write, years later 'one only dies from the first man'.

# 6

## *The Innocent Libertine*

Strangely enough, the tyrannical Willy cried easily. Colette herself had once seen him weeping at Bayreuth and he was seen in
tears after their marriage ended. She herself seems to have been
confused, apologetic and frightened judging from a letter quoted
by Madeleine Raaphorst-Rousseau and described as 'in the hands
of a bibliophile'. Colette wrote to the man who was still legally
her husband : 'I realize the seriousness of my mistake, and now
that I am alone I feel I cannot resign myself to living without
you, and this is with the deep awareness of everything that you
have done for me.' She still used the intimate '*tu*'. In her own
record she reported alternate states of desolation and courage
combined with fear of messages from Willy. He seems to have
tried hard to keep their professional relationship alive, either
because it was profitable to both of them or because it had become a habit to 'supervise' his wife – or even because he wanted
to give a good impression to the outside world.

In *Trois . . . Six . . . Neuf*, which was published in 1944, she
remembered some aspects of life in the rue de Villejust, where
there was a shady courtyard leading to the avenue du Bois. One
room was sunny enough to banish memories of the rue Jacob and
the other dark or somehow unsatisfactory places where she had
spent her years as a wife and a ghost-writer. At least part of the
time in her new home she chose to remember that she had been

surprisingly happy. 'I had never in my life lived alone. From the first night I spent in that ground-floor apartment I forgot the key in the outside of the lock. This wasn't mere negligence, but confidence. I never trusted a roof as much as I did that one. ... Borne up at times by a novel gaiety, at others cradled in a boundless, unreasoning security, I only know that I wanted to live and die there.' Unfortunately for her the American lady who owned the property told her that it was scheduled for demolition and that she would of course receive compensation. She wanted not money but her first home : 'Although condemned, it was nonetheless this ground-floor apartment that I trusted – deaf to summer storms, sealed off from winter hurricanes – because of its illusory character as a place of asylum, with the hope of guarding secretly there, one day, a happiness that would at last be mine.'

Everyone looks, or thinks they look, for happiness, and Colette's search for it was all the more poignant because it seemed perpetually to elude her. The difficulty she found in grasping it came sometimes dangerously near to not wanting it. People, happiness, friendship, love : the ingredients of life. She felt she needed them, but was not always sure how to find them. In describing the rue de Villejust apartment Colette mentions a visiting cat and the women who rode by early in the morning on their way to the Bois. Life had consisted too much of people who were on the horizon, on their way somewhere else.

Colette may have been temporarily disillusioned about men by 1906, when she and 'the first man' were divorced. In spite of her cool remarks later about women like Renée Vivien it was a woman at this point who brought her emotional happiness. Inevitably it had been Willy who introduced her to the strange and no doubt unhappy woman known either as the Marquise de Belboeuf or the Marquise de Morny.

'Known as' because 'Missy', youngest daughter of the Duc de Morny, had been already divorced from the Marquis. Her background had perhaps hardly prepared her for happiness. The legendary Duc de Morny was the illegitimate son of Hortense de Beauharnais, wife of Louis Bonaparte, King of Holland; Morny, blood-brother of Napoleon III, was a brilliant and cunning man who had met the eccentric Princess Troubetzkhoi while French ambassador to Russia. He brought her back to France, where they married, and, although not happy together, had four children. The Duchesse did not care for children and the youngest, christened Mathilde, but always referred to as 'Missy', she thought particularly displeasing. She found her ugly, called her 'the tapir', and although the Duc enjoyed the child's company she allowed the girl to be brought up mainly by servants and in Spartan fashion. When Morny died he had the most splendid funeral of the century and his widow, at least pretending to be distraught, cut off her hair and it was buried with him. Soon afterwards she married a Spanish duke.

By 1906 'Missy', who was interested in the theatre, was a good friend to Colette. The two women wanted to appear on the stage together and in the autumn of that year Colette wrote to Georges Wague asking if he could give lessons to the Marquise, who wanted to play the rôle of Franck in the mime-drama *Rêve d'Egypte*. She was so close to Missy at the time that when not in her own apartment she was at Missy's house in the rue Georges-Ville, 'A child of seven months knows that'. The drama in question had been written jointly by Wague himself, Emile Vuillermoz and the man who was still so near, Willy himself. Wague agreed to give the lessons and in November the two women were ready to appear in private, not yet in *Rêve d'Egypte* but in another mime-drama *La Romanichelle*. Indispensable as background to Colette's suddenly active life are the *Lettres de la Vagabonde* published in 1961. The editor of these letters, Claude Pichois, has added to them an article by Fernand Hauser published in *Le Journal* on 17th November, 1906 which demands to be quoted. When the reporter called at Missy's house the first thing he heard was Colette's voice saying that he could, to use equivalent slang, go and jump in the lake. She told him he was indiscreet, that the performance was to be in private for the members of a club and had nothing to do with the newspapers.

'A man, dressed entirely in velvet, holding a palette in his hand, entered : this man was the Marquise in the costume for her part in *La Romanichelle.*'

Colette told the reporter that it amused her, 'one amuses oneself as best one can. But why tell your readers that? I can't allow . . .'

'At this moment Willy, author of *Claudine à l'école*, came in :

"Marquise," he said, "since an editor from *Le Journal* is in your house, there's no point in showing resistance; he'll know very well how to make you talk, and, if he doesn't get a picture from you, he'll know how to get one all the same. . . ." '

The Marquise looked alarmed, but controlled herself and talked. She explained that her stage appearances in Paris were limited to performances in private and for these occasions she had adopted the name of Yssim, a transparent alias if ever there was one. She admitted she had acted in Spain and danced the fandango in Tangiers. She was hesitant when asked if she had thought of acting in public, at which point Colette took charge of the situation and dictated to the journalist : 'Write : "She does not intend to", and emphasized each syllable.' Then the fortunate journalist was allowed to watch a rehearsal.

'We sat in a dining-room with old furniture and valuable hangings, in the presence of a marble bust of Napoleon I; a pianist sat down at the piano, Georges Wague watched'; the journalist sat in a corner with Willy. 'The two artistes played their parts with equal mastery; this rehearsal was the last but one before the performance. And I admired the ease with which the Marquise wore her man's costume and acted her rôle; we felt we were watching a professional mime; she is in fact perfect. . . .'

Willy congratulated both 'Yssim' and Colette. Then, as the latter made eyes at him he said 'When Madame was married to me she didn't look at me like that!'

Everyone laughed, and this remark seems to sum up both Colette's first marriage and its aftermath.

In spite of Missy's reluctance to admit that she might act in public, she was obviously tempted and in November 1906 the newspaper *L'Intransigeant* announced that she would appear at the Théâtre Marigny in *Pan* by Charles van Lerberghe with music by Robert Haas. Colette was to play Paniska and her costume consisted of 'a few animal skins'. But Missy may have had stage-fright, for she apparently withdrew at the last moment and handed over her rôle to Georges Wague. Unfortunately the public assumed she had appeared and Wague found that people who did not know him mistook him for Missy in the street. It is clear from surviving photographs that the Marquise looked like a man, and a not very happy one. Colette herself was photographed in men's clothes, sometimes holding a cigarette with well-posed detachment. She took care later, in *Le Pur et l'impur*, to deny any ambitions towards masculinity : '... how shy I was, how much of a woman I was beneath my shorn hair, when I pretended to be a young man!'

Once her divorce was final Colette seems to have found within herself that energy and enthusiasm which characterized the rest of her life. Her letters show her organizing people and events. At the same time her stage performances caused interest at many levels; people came to the theatre and the music-hall to see Willy's ex-wife, or Missy's 'friend' but many of them were impressed by other qualities that were to become identified with Colette. It was quite clear that whatever the circumstances which had brought her to the stage and whatever the degree of her talent, she gave herself wholly to her new career. She studied her rôles conscientiously and Georges Wague has been quoted many times on the subject of her over-punctuality at rehearsals, for out of sheer anxiety she would always arrive too soon. The most important quality however was her indefinable detachment and *pudeur*, which can only half satisfactorily be translated as 'modesty'. At least one critic wondered how the delightful and bourgeoise Madame Willy could have 'descended' so low as to perform in this type of entertainment. It was no 'descent' for her since she became involved only with the aspects which gave her personal and artistic pleasure. If the plots of these mime-dramas were absurd and melodramatic, she was unconcerned; if she had to reveal her breasts, as in the famous piece *La Chair*, this was because the theme demanded it. Was she anxious to regain, or even gain for the first time, her confidence as a woman by appearing in public in a series of erotic or revealing costumes? Possibly. She appeared in this type of entertainment for five or six years. Earlier she had written dramatic criticism with Willy, later she wrote it again, seriously and on her own. Later too she was to appear occasionally, with partial success, as a serious actress. In the meantime the music-hall stage brought her good friends, some sort of income, a feeling of independence.

Inevitably she became involved in scandal, 'inevitably' because in the case of Colette it tended to happen. She had no faculty for assessing how other people would react to what she did; neither is it true that she 'did not care'. She tended to be unconcerned and did what she wanted to do. It seems unlikely for instance that she and Missy wanted to shock the public by their joint appearance in *Rêve d'Egypte* for which Wague had 'groomed' the Marquise. The theme of the *Rêve* was based on the story of an Egyptian mummy which slowly awakens and gracefully unwinds its 'bandages'. The fashion of the moment was to cause just enough shock to fill the theatre, and in January 1907 the management of the Moulin-Rouge obviously hoped for just such a result. In any case Colette was still haunted by her ex-husband, and everyone knew his tastes. What everyone had forgotten was that Missy had an ex-husband too.

The Marquis de Belboeuf was not pleased to hear that the Marquise was appearing on the stage and that in this particular drama she and Colette were to exchange a prolonged and passionate kiss. He and his friends from the Jockey Club attended the première in an angry mood and when the ubiquitous Willy tried to lead the applause he was forced to leave the theatre by an emergency exit. The Morny family joined in next day and asked the police to ban the show. It went on by means of two expedients – its name was changed to *Songe d'Orient* and the unlucky Missy again abdicated in favour of Wague. There was a rumour that the Government of Egypt had contemplated diplomatic action, and the drama was removed from the Moulin-Rouge repertoire. Colette was interviewed and complained angrily to journalists that the Jockey Club members had behaved miserably. She said that it was 'not in her nature' to have stage fright. The scenes in the theatre did not frighten her either and she intended to continue her career. She hoped she would not be forced to go abroad to earn her living.

If Colette's music-hall years had prevented her from writing then she might have been criticized for taking up the 'profession of those without a profession', as she called it. She did go on writing, and for this much credit is due to Missy. In spite of Colette's many brave words about being 'alone' she rarely, after the summers at Les Monts-Boucons, experienced solitude. She needed to have people close to her, and perhaps one person closer than any other. Missy's house in Paris and her villa at Le Crotoy on the baie de Somme were open to her. The relationship between the two women is perhaps best described as *amitié amoureuse*, a term much more expressive than 'lesbianism', of which there is no simple definition. The prose piece *Nuit Blanche* included in the collection of essays *Les Vrilles de la vigne*, dedicated to 'M', who is assumed to be Missy, illuminates the friendship, with all its emotional and physical depth. When two women are deeply fond of each other, or are at least drawn together by some irresistible force which can only be described as sexual, the relationship can sometimes resemble that of husband and wife and sometimes that of parent, usually mother and daughter. There can be more than one type of relationship and within its varying framework the two rôles can sometimes be interchangeable. The lyrical *Nuit Blanche* is about two people who share a bed, but it is not until the last sentence that grammatical details make it clear who the people are – two women. 'You will give me pleasure, leaning over me, your eyes filled with maternal anxiety, you who seek, through your passionate woman friend, the child you did not have. . . .'

When Colette decided to undertake exhausting theatrical tours of provincial towns with the famous Tournées Baret, Missy often went with her. All Colette's experiences on these tours, depressing, comical or heartening, went into her novel *La Vagabonde*, the sketches of *L'Envers du Music-Hall* and other writing, but alongside the praise and appreciation of good friends like Wague and the other artistes, there is no reference to Missy. It is only Colette's letters at the time which reveal her presence in the background. Missy gave her a splendid fountain pen and 'exciting loose-leaf notebooks with ruled pages'. When Missy was with her in Brussels in 1908 Colette admitted how comforting her friend's companionship was. 'But I've been so tired! And then, taking advantage of Missy's reassuring presence, I've had a real attack of 'flu, sudden and violent. When Missy is there I allow myself every luxury.' Colette was in Brussels acting the name part in *Claudine*, the play which had originally been adapted by Willy from the first two books in the series. She had remodelled the play herself 'in an autobiographical direction' and although she seems to have been successful she cannot have been too pleased by the appearance of Willy, who made unkind remarks from the wings.

Although Colette did not publish any work during 1906, the year of her divorce, she was rarely idle, in spite of her new profession and the new turning in her own life. The essay collection *Les Vrilles de la vigne* shows that she had adjusted equally to a new situation, for in addition to the pieces dedicated to Missy there is one written for Willy and one for his new companion, later wife, Meg Villars. This couple often stayed at a villa at Le Crotoy on the baie de Somme very near the villa Belle-Plage owned by Missy.

*Les Vrilles de la vigne* was a curious book, belonging like *La Retraite Sentimentale* to this period of transition, full of prose-poetry which recalls Willy's much-quoted remark 'Have I married the last of the lyric poets?' It also contains the revealing piece called *Le Miroir* in which Colette finally disassociates herself from Claudine – or thinks she does so. Its title is significant, for if Willy's vanity often led him to look in the mirror, Colette was no less fascinated by herself. Later, when less preoccupied perhaps by her own reflection, real or unreal, her writing constantly includes acute and detailed descriptions of women – she was intrigued by the many facets of their appearance, and never grew tired of looking at them.

The stage also fascinated Colette; she wrote and performed in 1909 an amusing little comedy *En Camarades* in which the leading parts were played by herself and her dog. Its admirers included no less a figure than Léon Blum. She enjoyed the mime-drama *La Chair*, was sorry when she could not go to the States to play it in New York, told Wague she would act in it wherever she could. With all due respect to Georges Wague the scenario was pure melodrama: the beautiful Yulka lives with her lover Hokartz in a smugglers' cabin near the Austro-Hungarian frontier. He comes home to find her in the arms of a rival, Yorki, drives the latter away and rages against Yulka. Her dress is torn, revealing her breasts. Hokartz is overwhelmed, asks to be forgiven but is rejected. In furious despair he nails his hand to the table with his dagger. Yulka tries to flee, but when she sees what Hokartz has done she places her hand on his. With his free arm he tries to embrace her. He dies and she loses her reason. The title, for those who need a translation, means simply *Flesh*.

Colette was much photographed when she was a mime, but how those eloquent poses were translated into action is a matter for conjecture, for contemporary opinions vary to an intriguing extent.

'. . . she danced in mime drama', wrote André Rouveyre, 'and danced it in the nude. This was a sorry exhibition. For, if Colette already had her spiritual wings, she did not succeed on the stage in lending them to her body. No more had she a deep sense of choreographic drama, which in some dances can take place in relative immobility. But, apparently Colette as a dancer was not concerned with originality, suitability, or any other difficult or severe research in dancing. Her mimicry and actions were in silhouette according to the professional tradition of mime. But she lacked even the elementary preparation for the profession, also any serious initiation in facial expression, down to the modest but sound recourse of the elementary simplification of important attitudes and gestures. In fact, everything which could animate a grotesque show in the diffuse theatre lighting.

'Under the pretext of some faun-like mime of the Catulle Mendès type, she tried to leap without anything aerial or significant in her movement. Every time she came down after a leap her bare feet resounded heavily with a flat sound of the heel and the sole of the foot on the cold stage, while her legs bent slightly in reaction, thereby subduing it.'

He went on to point out that Colette's performances were typical of the times.

'There was much ignorance and presumption concerning the art of the dance, which after all is a little more difficult than playing with a skipping rope. But this was the moment of juvenile and inconsequent performances. Elsewhere in Paris you could see and hear Tiarko Richepin jumping on the piano with his feet tied together to show the originality of his music, while

Sacha Guitry gave lectures with his mouth full of sandwiches, drowned in the dispute between words and saliva. Everyone thought himself a genius, and that was enough to magnify everyone's ideas, even the most inopportune. Colette's nudity, which was bold for the time, and her spontaneous attack on dancing and mime were obviously a mistake, but it showed us all the more her authenticity as a writer, and the exclusive, inviolable presence of genius in her books.'

It is only fair to add that Rouveyre published these remarks some fourteen years after Colette left the stage. His memories of her as a mime and a dancer must surely have been faint, and overlaid by his knowledge of her as a writer. However, the critic Louis Delluc wrote appreciatively in *Comoedia Illustré* about Colette's performance with Colette the author in mind.

'For me, the most original of the mimes, and the most true, is Colette. She is a vagabond, she scatters her talent around in outbursts which are works of art. But in everything that she does she remains herself and the mime remembers the spontaneous and incisive writer. *La Chair!* She would willingly name the whole of her lived and living work by this title. She has celebrated the dominating and treacherous flesh, the worn-out or triumphant flesh, the sacred flesh, but gradually she moves higher, she becomes purer, she sees things beautifully, she will see things greatly. Her plastic poses are those of an intellectual woman, but there is nothing strange or wearisome about them. She gives at the same time the impression of daring and naiveté, there is something chaste in her face; is it the mouth, the eyes or the forehead? There is also something which is obviously sensuous, but there again she does not know what. All of her is like this. She makes play with a large white veil in which she envelops and drapes herself, where she moulds her own shape; she has perfect legs and feet. Then she reveals her uplifted bosom, and then the whole of her harmonious nudity, and we do not know if we are disturbed or if we simply wonder at her. For she tries to be moving, and, possibly, perverse, and we let ourselves be dominated by her wishes, but we feel that in all this there is something inexplicable and something very pure.'

In this way the image of Colette as the 'innocent libertine' was formed. She herself may not have taken the music hall seriously, but it was her escape from the locked writing room, and its artificiality was more valid than the pretence of her marriage. After all the descriptions of Colette as a mime one of the funniest was written by herself in 1946, when she looked at old photographs: 'I reserve my keenest pleasure for a photograph where my good friend Georges Wague threatens my breast with a knife which is, at the very least, Catalan. I drop my eyes, I half open my mouth for a (silent) cry, but I don't forget, despite the urgency, to bring my left leg forward, knee slightly bent, in the manner of a *diseuse à voix*; Georges Wague ... reveals ... an unparalleled ferocity of gaze. He is going to stab this proffered breast – this pretty breast. .... But because the space is limited he has more the air of intending to tattoo his touching victim with the point of the dagger. ...'

She finished *La Retraite sentimentale* which she had started some time before her divorce and it was published in 1907. This was Claudine's last appearance in a novel, but part of her had become Colette. It is Colette who describes the house and garden with such intense and loving nostalgia, and Colette who goes a stage further than the two heroines of *Claudine s'en va* in learning independence. Claudine's husband Renaud is ill and dies. The devotion and loyalty Claudine displays are another proof that Colette was writing, as several people have thought, of an ideal marriage, the marriage she might have dreamt of when she was eighteen. Later, she dismissed Renaud as 'hollow'; there was perhaps nothing else she could do. The book shows clearly how Colette 'grew up'. She was still capable of making Claudine try to push the homosexual Marcel and the promiscuous Annie into each other's arms. Maugis appears, too, for the last time, and there is an odd description of Colette's own appearance on the stage, for which she gives herself the somewhat comic name of Willette Collie. Colette sent a copy of the novel to Marguerite Moreno who was in South America. When she replied, Moreno asked her friend tactfully if she was 'content', adding that she would not use the word 'happy'.

It was Missy who perhaps at this period brought Colette more 'contentment' than anyone else. For with Missy by her side she gave the impression of being both confident and happy. When Roger Peyrefitte wrote *L'Exilé de Capri* he chose to say in it that Colette wore bracelets engraved with the words, 'I belong to Missy'. He also quoted a couplet 'composed' by Willy:

> *Son nom n'a pas de sexe, quoi qu'on sache,*
> *Puisqu'on dit beau pour boeuf et belle pour la vache*

and it is tasteless and unfunny enough to be genuine. If Missy was in some strange way a mother figure, compensating for the absence of a real mother, what had happened to Sido? She had written to Colette in 1908 in some surprise about her new career. 'You're going into the theatre *pour tout de bon*, so you must enjoy it and earn money, no doubt. Well, I never imagined you were suited to it, for you were rather all in one piece – and for the stage one needs to be so supple, from both a physical and moral point of view, so I didn't really see that you had these qualities.' She added one more sentence: 'You've become more adaptable in both ways, it's true.'

Captain Colette had died some time previously and been buried with his Zouave's cloak draped over the coffin. His daughter seems to have realized much later in life that she had hardly known him. Her husband had been much older than herself, her men friends too, and at this period when she could have felt disorientated she was lucky enough to know the self-effacing Léon Hamel, recipient of most of the *Lettres de la Vagabonde* published in 1961. He was fifteen years older than she was and according to the brief and colourful evocation by Claude Pichois : *'Grand, élancé, très distingué d'allure, valseur tennisman, homme du monde, dilettante par vocation'*. Since his private fortune allowed him to live as he wished he had travelled widely and spent seventeen years in Egypt. Colette had dedicated to him one of the essays in the first edition of *Les Vrilles de la vigne* and later included him, with the barely disguised name of Hamon, in *La Vagabonde*. He apparently destroyed Colette's letters to him but only after carefully copying them into 'an exercise book similar to the manuscript of several works by Colette'.

About her novel *La Vagabonde* Colette, as usual, spoke little in her letters, but in September 1909 she wrote from Missy's villa to Hamel saying 'oh yes, there is one piece of news : the day before yesterday I began what will be, I hope, a kind of novel . . . I don't begin it without apprehension, I admit, and it makes me grumpy and nervy'. She revised it considerably, asked the editor of *La Vie Parisienne* to delay the serialization because she wanted it to be 'right', and was still working on the novel in the summer of 1910. This was the seventh novel she had written and the first to be completed without any supervision whatever from Willy. He had treated his ex-wife badly by selling the exclusive rights of the *Claudine* books to their original publisher, Ollendorff. The formerly submissive ghost-writer was angry enough about this to include a destructive portrait of Willy in *La Vagabonde*.

Nearly everyone Colette knew, and nearly everything she had done since 1906 went into this novel and biographers almost inevitably use its title for this chapter in her life. The heroine, Renée Néré, the unhappy actress disillusioned by marriage, is Colette herself. Brague, the actor-organizer is Georges Wague, Hamon is Hamel and the musician Taillandy, the ex-husband, is Willy. Colette was so angry with him that at one stage of the novel she forgot she had changed his profession and accidentally referred to the publishing royalties which he had skilfully kept for himself. The novel is well known, and so is the story of how it won only two votes when the members of the Académie Goncourt awarded their annual prize in 1910. The same number of votes went to Apollinaire's *L'Hérésiarque et Cie* and it is usually assumed that if the Académie subsequently looked foolish it was because neither of these books were read by all its members.

*La Vagabonde* seems somewhat over-effusive now but it is fascinating for the degree to which it is a *roman à clef*, for the way in which the heroine looks for love but retreats from it when offered. In spite of Renée's complaints about the fatiguing aspects of her profession, there is no doubt that her creator, her other self as it were, throughly enjoyed a way of life for which she seemed brilliantly suited. Colette herself never enjoyed writing. She often looked, unsuccessfully, for an escape from it, which was one of the reasons she so enjoyed acting in the mime-dramas which now seem mere melodrama.

The saddest aspect of *La Vagabonde* is the impression that the heroine cannot accept love, sad because the note seems so personal and autobiographical. Could 'the first man' in fact have caused so much damage? Apparently he could. Willy himself was hurt by his ex-wife's obvious references to his behaviour and replied by including an unkind portrait of Colette in a novel entitled *Lélie fumeuse d'opium*. But Renée (or Colette) did not refuse love simply because of the past, but also because of the present, her own nature, an intolerable conviction that she and perhaps many women in 1910, could never, like Millamant, 'dwindle into a wife'.

Colette's personal life was no longer limited only to her friendship with Missy, although this continued steadily for the time being; the generous Marquise had bought and furnished a villa for her in Brittany named Rozven, between Saint-Malo and Cancale. Colette had developed a near-fanatical love of the sea, although Sido warned her in 1910 to beware of bathing in cold

water. After so many exhausting journeys into the French provinces and Belgium Colette was able to travel for pleasure during
the winter of 1910–11. She had met Auguste Hériot, a young
man whose family owned the Grands Magasins du Louvre; he
is thought to be the 'Max' of *La Vagabonde*, he took her by train
to Italy, which she had never seen. Letters about Naples and
Roman ruins came to Léon Hamel, followed by a revealing
remark about Hériot: 'My little companion sends you his best
wishes. He's a nice boy when he's alone with me. He'll never be
happy, he's built on a foundation of sadness.'

After Italy Colette came to Nice, still with Hériot and joined
by a young woman named Lily de Rême. It was Hamel who
received descriptions of their life together which sounded like the
raw material for more novels: ... 'the trio we make up would
interest you. These two children in love with me are strange –
through the mere fact of loving me. I feed them up and make
them sleep. My *amour-propre* finds maternal satisfaction in their
appetites and their clear complexions.' Colette herself, now, had
reached her maturity, yet how much she still needed her confi-
dant Hamel! 'But I'm not very pleased with the young H(ériot).
How often have I hesitated to talk to you about him! And to
whom could I talk frankly about this, if not you? The die is
cast, it's you I will ask for secrecy and advice, for the incident
seems to me serious especially for him, I'm not in any moral
danger. I shall have to talk to you.' This was written from Tunis,
and in the next letter she mentions that Hériot was 'making up'
to Missy.

When she herself returned to France she went straight to
Rozven where the solicitous Missy, who was not pleased with
Colette's general state, had worked miracles to prepare bedrooms
for them both. It was to Louis de Robert, a friend of Proust's,
that Colette wrote in April 1911 telling how she had rushed
back to 'take refuge in Missy, to be scolded, looked after and
given warmth'. Rozven was wonderful, the fishing was good,

Missy was taming a chaffinch and had chapped hands through working in the garden.

The following month there was trouble between Missy and Colette, but it did not last long. Missy was also training a crow now, feeding the birds on ants' eggs. In July 1911 a new name appeared in one of Colette's letters: Sidi.

# 7

## *The Secret Woman*

The name sounded frivolous but it was merely an affectionate diminutive; its owner was someone whose background at least was far from frivolous, the Baron Henri de Jouvenel des Ursins, who was co-editor of the important Paris daily paper *Le Matin* and lived whenever he could at the family château Castel-Novel near Varetz in the Corrèze. In 1911 he was thirty-five, divorced from Claire Boaz, by whom he had a son, Bertrand de Jouvenel, later well known as a writer on international affairs and political theory. Henri de Jouvenel himself was an exceptionally attractive man who was assumed to have a brilliant future. He was not unattached, for everyone in Paris knew about his liaison with Madame de Comminges, by whom he had a second son, Renard, also destined to enter politics.

By the time Colette first mentioned 'Sidi' in a letter to Léon Hamel (2nd July, 1911) she was obviously close to him. Everything was going 'too well', but she was anxious about Missy's 'mental state'. Two months earlier Colette had written to Wague from Rozven saying 'what an arrival! It's hard – it can be sorted out – but it's hard. I'll tell you about it.' She hoped Wague would ask her to come to Paris for rehearsals, for she wanted an excuse to leave the house Missy had furnished for her with such care. For the second time things settled down, but the month of July contained so many melodramatic events that even Colette, who wrote letters so easily, had no time to write, not even to her friend Hamel and not even to her mother. She had admittedly been on tour in Switzerland with Wague and Christine Kerf playing in the inevitable mime drama *La Chair*, but during the last few years these tours had not stopped her from writing both letters and books.

The two men with whom she was involved, Auguste Hériot, who was already in the past, and Henri de Jouvenel who was forcibly in the present, preoccupied her in different ways. Hériot, whom she usually referred to as 'le petit', sent her letters and telegrams, but as a matter of principle she did not reply or else put him off with lies. De Jouvenel was different from the men Colette had met so far for in simple terms he was a man of action, unlike Willy, Marcel Schwob and the other writers she knew. He also wrote very well, but his writing stemmed from action and was action in itself. He had recently been involved in a dramatic incident concerned not with his personal life but with the paper of which he was co-editor. An anonymous article in the other important Parisian daily, *Le Journal*, had attacked *Le Matin*. De Jouvenel decided to challenge his rival editor to a duel, but Henri Letellier, director of *Le Journal,* refused to accept the challenge. De Jouvenel then published a letter on the front page of *Le Matin* which included the uncompromising sentence, 'Cowardice, when it reaches the level you have seen today, attains a kind of perfection'. After further exchanges of witnesses Henri de Jouvenel and Georges Barlet, the editorial secretary of *Le Journal*, fought it out with revolvers at a cycle-racing track near Paris. At the first shots both men were wounded in the forearm and the fight was stopped, but de Jouvenel at least could not use one arm for some time.

In the years leading up to 1914 such incidents were not as rare in Paris as one might imagine. Henri de Jouvenel, who was in any case much talked about, was still thought to be the lover of Madame de Comminges, and this lady was known to some as 'la Panthère', the Panther. He had perhaps not yet realized that he was in love with Colette. Missy was jealous of him and in any case she was fond of Hériot, so fond indeed that she had made plans involving both him and Colette. At the end of that melodramatic July the only plans destined to succeed were those made by Henri de Jouvenel.

At the end of July Colette wrote to Léon Hamel a letter which is the raw material of biography. It is long, breathless, radiant, in its way selfish, for she had reached a crucial moment in her life. Happiness, as she wrote, was within her reach, and after so many years spent as a 'prisoner' or a 'vagabond', she was not going to let it elude her. Other people's happiness or unhappiness no longer concerned her very much. She could not allow anything or anyone, rivals or admirers, to stand in her way. If for a short period she had felt the need to protect herself against the inevitably related states of happiness and love she now went out aggressively to take hold of them. From this moment on Colette was ready to organize her own life, the time when others had organized it for her was long past. Her 'own life' however was no longer a solitary one in the midst of friends and work, it was now inextricably involved with the man she loved.

The events of that hot July of 1911 would have needed considerable dilution before supplying themes for several highly melodramatic novels. Few novelists would have expected their readers to believe such a story, and Colette herself was the first to suggest to Hamel that the events were 'too theatrical'. And so they were. In this letter Colette used only initials to refer to the 'protagonists'. 'J' of course is de Jouvenel and 'M' is Missy. 'P' is 'The Panther'. 'S' and 'S' stand for Sauerwein and Sapène of *Le Matin*. Paul Barlet was a friend whom Colette had met *aux ateliers*, while working for Willy.

Dear Hamel, [she wrote from Rozven on 31st July, 1911]
I am absolutely full of dismay and remorse for having worried

you. At the same time I've also worried Mama and the people who loved me, by leaving them in ignorance about my fate.

Dear Hamel, so many things have happened! I have been unhappy, was it necessary to pay for happiness (let's touch wood), yes, something resembling happiness that I can see gleaming very near, within my reach? (I'm touching wood desperately!)

I reached Rozven this morning after a very hectic month spent almost entirely in Paris, during that dreadful heat. Do you know that I'd been acting in Geneva and Lausanne? Did you know that the day after his duel J landed in Lausanne, badly wounded and his arm in plaster, declaring that he couldn't and wouldn't live without me any longer? Do you know that at the same time H wanted to rejoin me in Switzerland and that I prevented him from doing so by means of frantic lying and contradictory telegrams? Do you know that on returning to Paris J admitted to the P that he was in love with another woman? At that she declared she would kill that woman, whoever she was. In desperation J transmitted this threat to me, to which I replied 'I'll go and see her'. And I went to see her. And I said to the P 'I'm the woman'. At that she collapsed and pleaded with me. Short-lived weakness, for two days later she announced to J her intention to do me in. Desperate again, J had me kidnapped by S in a motor-car and accompanied me, still with S, to Rozven where we found M icy and disgusted, having just been informed through the P. Then my two guardians left me and Paul Barlet mounted guard, revolver in hand, beside me. M, still icy and disgusted, beat a retreat to Honfleur. Soon afterwards (three days), J called me back to him by telephone and S came to take me by car, because the P was lurking about in the hope of finding me, also armed with a revolver. Then began a period of semi-sequestration in Paris, where I was guarded like a valuable shrine by the Sûreté and also by J, S and S, those three pillars of *Le Matin*. And believe me or not, this period has just come to an end, concluded by an unexpected, providential and magnificent event! Tired of all this carrying-on Monsieur Hériot and Madame la P have just embarked on the yacht *Esmerald* for a cruise of at least six weeks, after astounding Le Havre, the home port, by some incredible drunken orgies. Is this good? Is it drama? rather too much so, isn't it?

In the meantime J distinguished himself by some very proper actions, which earned him the disapproval of M; for basically M adores H, she had prepared a room for him here, and she had intended to impose him on me in a kind of conjugal manner. It didn't need that to put me off this young man for ever. What more shall I tell you, dear Hamel! J is having his house arranged for me. He has no fortune, he has *Le Matin* (forty or so thousand francs) and since I earn my living well, we'll get by. Need I tell you again that I love this man, he's affectionate, jealous, unsociable and incurably honest? It's not necessary. I would very much like to see you. And I shall see you often, if you will agree to it, for J has already declared that he would allow me 'only Hamel and Barlet' Ah!

I'm glad to tell you also that S has revealed himself an incomparable person for J and for me – I'll tell you that. It was a very pleasant surprise.

M has bought Princesse, the villa which is 3 kilometres away from here. This piece of news sounds like an epilogue, doesn't it? The day after tomorrow I leave by car for Castel-Novel, J's château in the Corrèze, I'll send you a photograph of the place ... M is still icy and disgusted, and whatever I do I can't get a sensible word out of her. I assure you. It's not unkindness on my part, it makes me very unhappy. ...

Some chapters in Colette's life read like a parody of one of her novels, but in none of her novels does half so much happen as in this letter. It is worthwhile remembering here that after the publication of *La Vagabonde* she had for the first time taken up regular journalism for *Le Matin* for which she wrote a weekly article. She tended to think of journalism, as of the music-hall, as the profession of those without a profession, but she had the energy for it and also the 'love of cataclysms' inherited from her mother. She became a contributor to *Le Matin* only with difficulty, for one of the senior editors had objected to her, saying that if this 'mountebank' joined the paper he would leave. She came however, and he remained. Her interest in journalism was parallel to her love of the stage, leading her to present each article in the form of a miniature drama with dramatis personae and suitable decor. Murder trials, flights in a balloon or an airship alternated with articles remarkable for their sense of movement – a description of the Tour de France, for example, or a scene among the crowd hoping to see the police capture the leader of the notorious Bonnot gang. At first these articles were signed only with a small mask, but eventually Colette's name appeared. These pieces were published in book form with the title *Contes des 1001 Matins* in 1970. The range of topics covered is wide and almost conceals two facts – that Colette only wrote about what she knew, replacing technical details by imaginative description, and was always delighted to write on any question involving women. This journalism occupied her soon after 1910 and three years went by without the publication of a new novel. This different type of writing allowed her to write, as usual, in a strongly personal vein but with a new approach. All the apparently objective descriptions are in fact deeply subjective; at the same time she rarely makes any direct statement in her own voice – her 'characters' speak for themselves and by implication for her. Fashion, slimming, physical culture, women attending lectures or meetings of the Congrès, young girls working in the theatre – she watched all this and enjoyed it, alternating criticism, surprise and praise.

Incredibly enough she still appeared on the stage in *La Chair*, the equally melodramatic *Oiseau de Nuit* and similar pieces which, without their association with Colette, might have long been forgotten, apart from historical exhibitions in France. It is not surprising that her letters sometimes include a remark that she is tired, but it is even more surprising that she found time to write them at all.

Her mother wrote to her from the country reminding her that 'journalism kills novelists'. Sido was old now, Colette wrote to her regularly and was able to tell her about the presence of Henri de Jouvenel. In a famous passage in *La Naissance du Jour* Colette reconstructs a discussion she had with her mother, who had been upset by her divorce and was now even more upset at the prospect of a second marriage. She thought that 'anything would be better than marriage', while realizing that any other arrangement 'was not done'. She also said she preferred the 'other one', for Minét-Cheri would write wonderful things with him. She pointed out the danger of being in love, for a woman in love gives the man all her 'most precious gifts'. She added that a new husband might make her unhappy and Colette called her Cassandra.

Colette was thinking not of marriage but of happiness. She lived with de Jouvenel at Passy, where the chalet in the rue Cortambert had somehow to be made more habitable; in the letters she wrote at the time she mentions discussions with plumbers, painters and mosaic-workers, describes a delightful old gaming-table on which she and 'Sidi' played bezique but adds that they still had no bedroom. The best description of this period was the one she included in *Trois ... Six ... Neuf* published in 1944, when she mentioned her own emotional upheaval. 'Keen happiness and stunning misfortune menaced me simultaneously ... I hesitated under their impact. I was so anxious to show the same respect and interest towards the one as the other. The period of my extraordinary homes dates from this extraordinary season of the heart.' There existed a strange parallelism between her emotional state and this chalet which looked like 'a piece of Swiss stage-setting' and according to a romantic legend had once housed 'a jealous painter infatuated with his model'. She could resist neither de Jouvenel nor the chalet, with its vines and acacias, and she described, many years afterwards, the moonlit night in June when she first entered it. 'I halted at the border of this enticement, this excessive charm, this ambush. Perhaps there was still time to retrace my steps. But already my host had appeared in front of me. . . .'

In the letters she wrote to her friends there was no trace of this hesitation, but it must have been there, although she was not conscious of it at the time. She was in love, she wanted to give her whole self but felt perhaps that for her there was no more difficult thing in the world. Her mother had warned her about the danger of giving away her 'precious gifts'. For Colette this was the moment for loving and giving, the moment when *le femme cachée*, the 'secret woman' in her was able to take part in real life, not merely stage life. She was the first to recognize this : 'I owe a great deal to the chalet at Passy. Under its balconies and its trefoils I led a really feminine life, marked by everyday curable sorrows, revolts, laughter and cowardice . . . There I worked, harried by the need for money, there I spent hours of idleness.' These few sentences bring out all the extremes in her nature which had now encountered the corresponding extremes of Henri de Jouvenel.

Their relationship was infinitely less lyrical than the surroundings of the chalet. They loved each other but they argued and fought; they worked hard but they spent freely, were so short of money that Colette even pawned a pearl necklace. In the early summer of 1912 they were enjoying a holiday in Normandy but by the end of June they were going through a crisis. Colette wrote to Hamel from Tours giving a résumé in dialogue form of four days of conversation :

J. – We must separate.

C. – Yes!

J. – Life together. . . .

C. – . . . is impossible.

J. – That doesn't stop us in any way from being good friends!

C. – On the contrary!

J. – So we're going to leave each other . . .

C. – At once!

J. – Oh! there's no hurry.

C. – Yes, yes, it's absolutely urgent.

J. – Absolutely isn't the word . . .

C. – Absolutely! great break-up on July 1st, each one goes his own way, and if on my side there's some change in my feelings, that's to say, if I meet someone bedworthy and likeable, mere honesty makes it a duty for me. . . .

J. – Certainly. But while waiting. . . .

C. – While waiting I'm going off to the rue La Fontaine.

J. – That's useless, stupid even. You're better off here.

C. – No. Goodnight, Sidi.

J. – But. . . . Where are you going?

C. – Where I have to. You yourself, you told me. . . .

J. – Oh! what I said isn't very important. . . . Wouldn't you like a game of bezique?

C. – One for the road? with pleasure.

J. – . . . Four thousand five hundred!

C. – Bravo! after that . . . goodbye Sidi.

J. – But . . . what are you doing this evening? If you don't object utterly to having dinner chez Laurent, outside. . . . The weather's fine, I so much want to stay with you! . . . etc. etc. etc. . . !

[The rue la Fontaine meant Paul Barlet's house.]


Colette added that this was the funny side of it all, but unfortunately there were others. She thought however that she had

reached, and passed, the lowest possible point and was glad that
*Le Matin* had sent her to Tours to report on a sensational murder
trial. She had found it hard to be so much in love, for she was no
longer used to being dominated. She wanted love, and didn't
want it. She loved, as Natalie Clifford Barney had said, either
too little or too much. She could not easily tolerate an emotional
situation now if she were not in control, which hardly made for
an easy relationship, for the balance was wrong. She comforted
herself with the thought that she might be strong enough to bring
the liaison to an end if she chose. Sidi had looked wretched when
he drove her to the station : 'You know, Hamel, I don't despair
of treating him as lightly as Hériot. I've been working hard these
days against myself and for my own salvation.' She needed Hamel
very much, and he was the only one to receive her confidences.
Even physical exhaustion failed to make her sleep 'and I don't
want to go on being so inferior'. She was resentful towards de
Jouvenel but 'Alas, I miss terribly the *presence* of an unworthy
being, his warmth, the sound of his voice, his lies, his childishness
and his silliness'.

She realized she must have a home of her own but she had
not even the money to move or travel. Some income came from
*Le Matin* and some from performances of *L'Oiseau de Nuit,*
more was due to come from Sidi, but not before the end of
August. He was away a good deal. They were still lovers and 'on
good terms' and they needed each other physically. They had
'good moments and miserable quarters of an hour'. In the meantime she worked on a new novel and played piano music by
Schumann. What was going to happen? Sidi came back after
a week's flying, seemed in a good mood and found her 'transformed'. She hardly dared hope his good humour would last but
she accepted 'a terrible ephemeral happiness which had its own
damnable price; you know what it means, after terrible hours
and weeks, the *presence* of the person who is essential. He

arranges "our" future and the ornaments on the sideboard with the same mentality.'

Sidi seemed in fact to need her so much that he would only allow her two or three days to visit her mother, who was 'intolerable', for she insisted on seeing her daughter. From Châtillon Colette wrote to another friend and added briefly 'mama isn't splendid, but she can still last, and that's all one can ask of her'. Mama had recently written to Henri de Jouvenel the famous and indeed over-quoted letter which was to be published in *La Naissance du jour*. He had invited her to stay with him and she had declined, because her rose cactus was about to flower. Since this only happened once every four or five years she realized that she would not see it again. Another and previously unknown letter clearly written about the same period (and first published in *Le Figaro Littéraire* in 1953) carries a different message: 'Your graceful invitation makes me decide to accept it for many reasons: among these reasons is one which I never resist: seeing my daughter's dear face and hearing her voice. Finally, that of knowing you and seeing as far as possible why she has thrown her bonnet over the windmill for you.' Sido added that she was leaving a gloxinia and a sedum about to flower in the care of her daughter-in-law who would be pleased to be rid of her mother-in-law. This is what the letter seems to say, for Sido was too old perhaps to attend to details of grammar. She died three weeks after her daughter had been to see her.

Less than a month later, on 27th September, Colette wrote to Hamel: 'Mother died the day before yesterday. I don't want to go to the funeral. I'm telling hardly anyone and I'm not wearing any external mourning. At the moment I'm fairly well. But I'm tormented by the ridiculous idea that I won't be able to write to Mother any more as I used to do so often. My brother down there will be very unhappy. I'm continuing to act in *L'Oiseau* and to live as usual, that goes without saying. But as always when a grief matters enough I have an attack of internal . . .

inflammation which is very painful.' She added that Sidi was being very nice to her, 'he's looking after my grief – which more- over I hardly ever show – in an affectionate and sensitive way.'

The mother so loved – apparently – had become someone to whom Colette wrote letters. For readers of Colette, Sido has survived also as someone who wrote letters. The relationship in fact seems to have been more literary than natural. During the mid-1920s Sido was to occupy a large place in Colette's writing and all her advice to her daughter, from the famous 'look' to 'what will you do with so many husbands?' has been endlessly quoted, often with a sentimentality that Colette herself never showed. She seems all the same to have searched, through the idealized writing about Sido, for a natural closeness which may never in fact have existed. Sido, who had known no mother herself and acquired two unsatisfactory husbands, had perhaps loved her daughter not wisely but too well – she had tried to keep her for herself, and had in fact almost succeeded.

Less than three weeks later Colette wrote to Hamel a gay, holiday letter from Castel-Novel saying that she had only good news to relate. At least three generations of the de Jouvenel family were there, and everyone was busy, Sidi visiting the farm, his mother playing tennis. There were informal political dinner parties, local excursions and an air of happiness. By the end of October, when Colette was again on tour in Switzerland with Wague and Christine Kerf, she realized she was pregnant.

Among the many memories included in her last book, *L'Etoile Vesper,* the account of the pregnancy is one of the most amusing and the most strange. She was more surprised than anyone, for she was nearly forty and had not yet accepted marriage, let alone motherhood. Her actor friends looked after her and she remem- bered this period as *'une longue fête'*. Colette and Sidi were married in Paris on 19th December at half-past four, with Hamel as one of their witnesses, and there were several days of cele- brations.

In the meantime, what had happened to the good friend who had been 'icy and disgusted'? 'You want news of Missy?' she asked her actress friend Christiane Mendelys. 'I haven't any, and she continues to keep everything that belongs to me. I like to benefit from exceptional treatment, and I shall be the first person to have seen "the marquise" demanding money from a woman whom she has left.' Colette kept the house, Rozven, that Missy bought for her, but her former friend removed the furniture from it.

Since Colette was forced temporarily to leave the stage but still needed to earn money she went on with the novel she had started in the early summer. At first she had called it *Le Raisin volé* and this title even appeared in the periodical where it was being serialized. Soon, however, its title became *L'Entrave* and soon also its creator began to work more slowly. Again it is *L'Etoile Vesper* which describes the race between the book and the baby. Early in July Colette de Jouvenel was born, her parents were utterly delighted with her and the serialization of the novel was temporarily halted for its author stopped writing it. Among all Colette's letters about her daughter – who resembled her father when she was young – one is particularly moving. 'My goodness, how little one knows oneself! I arrive quietly, I find this little thing in the drawing-room – and I burst into tears! No doubt it's very natural but I was very surprised. She looked so beautiful.'

As the little girl grew up, carefully supervised by her English nurse, the letters continually reflect the joy her mother found in her; Colette always noted signs of independence and freedom, for just as Sido had relished any likeness to herself, her daughter reacted in the same way. She enjoyed the little Colette so much that she apologized to Hamel for being so boring about her and could not understand how she had succeeded in 'creating, quite unconsciously, a creature who resembles Sidi so faithfully!'

In her seventies Colette thought again about the birth of the little girl. 'But the meticulous admiration I devoted to my daughter – I did not call it, I did not feel it, as love. I waited. I studied the charming authority of my young nurse.' She was slightly surprised to find that she did not turn into a 'besotted mother', and not even into an 'ordinary' one. She waited until the little Colette earned her name of 'Bel-Gazou' : 'Yet I only regained my equanimity when intelligible speech blossomed on those ravishing lips, when recognition, malice and even tenderness turned a run-of-the-mill baby into a little girl, and a little girl into my daughter.'

# 8

## *The Problem of Life* 'à deux'

After the happy interruption of the summer of 1913 *L'Entrave*
was eventually finished in September, although Colette wrote
that she 'despised' it; the conditions of its writing may have
affected its composition for the start is too slow, and the heroine
of *La Vagabonde,* now that she has become rich and idle, seems
at first much less interesting. However, as soon as she is engaged
in the inevitable, insoluble emotional struggle with Jean, who has
left her friend May for her, the reader is absorbed and reads
slowly in order to relish both the situations and the interpreta-
tions; the latter may be given by Renée but is surely dictated by
Colette : 'I think that at certain moments all women make the
same gestures; in front of a mirror, or beside clear water, passing
near velvety flowers, fabrics or fruit, they give way to their two
temptations, which are always the same : adorning themselves,
which is to offer, and touching, which is to take.' This novel is
full of remarks which show duality of motive and sometimes the
reversal of rôles within a relationship. There can for instance
be no end to the 'fatal game' which the lovers play : 'if he is the
mastiff, I am the cat at the top of the tree. . . .' This metaphor
recalls a remark by Natalie Clifford Barney made many years
ago about Colette. 'Her favourite companions : a dog and a cat –
as everyone knows – were no doubt chosen because of their
remarkable resemblance to their mistress. Was her nature not

made up of those two animal natures? Obedient and devoted to a master, but secretly making use of the wild animal instinct which escapes all domination.' Many of her heroines inherited the same tendency.

There is no doubt that Colette remembered in this novel her own state of mind before her second marriage, for her heroine sees love as a hazard which she wants to avoid and yet not avoid. Then comes the terrible gap when Jean leaves Renée, and at the very end the curious awareness in Renée's mind that she and her lover have changed rôles – Jean seems to have taken her place, 'he is the eager vagabond' while she is 'anchored' for ever.

After *La Vagabonde* and now *L'Entrave* two things became clear – Colette wrote with remarkable, poignant understanding of women, but her men characters seemed to exist only to allow the development of the women. Her heroines fell in love with shadows, symbols of all the qualities that made relationships so difficult. The non-heroes, the men like Brague or Masseau, so closely modelled on Wague and Masson, were much more convincing. Colette seemed to believe that reality and happiness could be found with friends, but not with lovers, as though love had to be transmuted into friendship before it could be tolerated.

Six years passed before Colette was able to complete or publish another novel, for the First World War temporarily changed her life without making it any less full. She continued to work in journalism, for by now it had become an important source of income for her. The description, later published in *Les Heures longues,* of how the outbreak of war affected the stunned population of Saint-Malo, has become famous: 'How could I forget that moment? It was four o'clock, a fine misty day in a seaside summer, the golden ramparts of the old town standing by the sea which looked green on the beach, blue on the horizon – children in red bathing suits leaving the beach to go for tea and walking up the stifled streets . . . And from the centre of the town came every commotion at once: the tocsin, the crying of

children ... there was a crowd around the beadle with the drum,
who was reading; nobody listened to what he read because we
knew what it was. Women broke away from groups of people,
running, stopped as though stricken, and then ran again, looking
as though they had crossed an invisible boundary, and rushed on
to the other side of life. Some of them wept with their mouths
open. Young boys grew pale and looked in front of them like
sleep-walkers. The car, in which we were, stopped, hemmed in
by the crowd, who clung to its wheels. People climbed on to it,
in order to see and hear better, came down without even having
noticed us, as though they had climbed up a wall or a tree; in a
few days, who will know if this is yours or mine?"

However Colette did not merely observe the war, she worked
for a time in an improvised hospital in Paris but since Henri de
Jouvenel was immediately mobilized her one ambition was to
follow him to the front, which in late 1914 was still possible. The
letters and articles she wrote from Verdun, where she stayed with
the wife of a junior officer, give a graphic account of bombing
and military action generally, without forgetting such develop-
ments as black-market activities. In later novels, particularly in
*Chéri,* she was to remember everything she had observed, from
courage to corruption, from tragedy to inescapably comic detail.
Her status as a reporter was so eminent that in 1915 she was sent
to Italy from where she wrote descriptions which were later to
fascinate Proust. Her husband was able to join her for brief
periods of leave and Hamel in Paris was kept up to date with
cheerful descriptions of the Italian lakes. Early in 1917 Sidi was
in Rome as a delegate to the conference held by the Allies following certain peace proposals which had been made by the
Germans to President Wilson.

Naturally she spent many months of the war alone or with
her small daughter and women friends at Passy – until one day
a corner of the chalet fell into the garden during a thunder
shower. She then bought a house in the boulevard Suchet at

Auteuil and again, much later, she described it in *Trois . . . Six . . . Neuf.* To her surprise and delight the owner from whom she bought it – complete with batik hangings – was the once-famous actress Eve Lavallière whom she had known when she was young.

On the whole Colette had had an adventurous and not too harrowing war. In Italy a silent film was made of *La Vagabonde* and early in 1917 she had an encouraging experience at the British Embassy in Rome, where she read three of her animal monologues with outstanding success. 'The British Embassy here consoles me for the French one. Good informal people, a free life, home-made butter, incomparable garden, children . . . who make me jealous! Luminous, free, intelligent English children, and good food.' During the summer of 1917 however Colette was anxious about Sidi, of whom she had no news, but all was well in the end and life became almost normal again, with time away from Paris spent happily at Castel-Novel or Rozven.

During the war Colette had written many articles, published as *Les Heures longues* in 1917, while the previous year had seen *La Paix ches les bêtes.* The only full-length book which she completed at this period was the famous *Mitsou* which was serialized in 1917, after she had lost the manuscript in the Métro and been forced to write it all again. She described to Georges Wague how much this upset her – in spite of the warm September day she shivered so much from frustration that she was forced to go to bed with a hot-water bottle.

*Mitsou,* which has been much praised, is partly in dialogue form and at first seems to go back to the world of *La Vagabonde.* It concerns a young actress who is kept by a respectable middle-aged man until she falls in love with a soldier on leave. Mitsou is typical of the young women whom Colette admired for working hard and furthering their careers, but she furnished her apartment in pathetically bad taste. Admittedly, Mitsou's discovery of love and the letters she writes, have charm, but this is one of the few books where Colette comes near to sentimentality. Mitsou and her 'blue lieutenant' are like people seen through gauze curtains in some scene from a fairyland ballet. However, *Mitsou* marks one important development in technique, for there is no first-person narrative and although the theatrical background is part of Colette's experience, she herself is absent from the novel. It would be unfair not to quote the letter, with its long sentences and parentheses, which Proust wrote to Colette after reading the book.

I have just found this letter I wrote over six weeks ago. I am sending it to your publisher since I cannot find your address. Again I send you my respectful admiration.

> 102, boulevard Haussman (provisionally), for the house has been bought by a banker, who wants to make it into a bank and give notice to all the tenants.

Madame,

I wept a little this evening, for the first time for a long time, and yet for some time I have been full of sorrow, suffering and worry. But the reason I wept was not due to that at all, but to reading Mitsou's letter. The two last letters are the chef-d'oeuvre of the book (I mean of *Mitsou,* for I have not yet read *En camarades,* my eyes are very bad, I cannot read quickly). Perhaps, if it were absolutely necessary in order to show you that I am sincere in my praise, to tell you something I would not allow to be called criticism, directed toward a Master like yourself, I would find that this letter from Mitsou is so beautiful, but also a little too pretty, because amongst so much that is admirable and profoundly natural there is just a touch of preciousness. Indeed, when, in the restaurant (in the amazing restaurant, to which I compare with a little humiliation my innumerable inferior restaurants, sodoms which you do not yet know, and which will appear gradually) (in the restaurant which makes me also think with a little melancholy of this dinner which we were to have together and which, like everything else in my life since that time – and for a long time before – could never happen), the blue lieutenant speaks of a nice wine which tastes of coffee and violets, this is so much within the character and language of the blue lieutenant. (In this restaurant, how I love the wine waiter, with his dreamy haughtiness, etc!) But for Mitsou, there are in her letter things which would have seemed to me far too pretty if I had not found from the beginning (like you, is it not?) that Mitsou is far more intelligent than the blue lieutenant, that she is admirable, that her momentary bad taste in furnishing has no importance. (I wish you could see my 'bronzes', it is true that I have simply kept them, and not chosen them), and that moreover the miraculous progress of her style, which is as rapid as hail, corresponds exactly with the title : How wit comes to young girls.

Madame, I wrote all that a fortnight ago, but there have been such ups and downs in my health, such serious ones, that I have not been able to finish my letter. Since things became better my first gesture is to beg you to accept my respectful admiration.

*Marcel Proust*

Perhaps Proust's mention of the word 'precious' was salutary, for she could hardly be accused of such a failing again. Seven years after the publication of *L'Entrave* came what may be her masterpiece, *Chéri*, in 1920.

Masterpiece because, especially when considered together with its sequel, *La Fin de Chéri*, published six years later, the book has such richness – a perceptive treatment of a classic sexual situation plus an account of social life which appears impartial but in the sequel especially contains deeply-implied criticism. A full-length study of these two books could concentrate on the complex relationship between a young man and an older woman and on the social conditions which produced the *demi-mondaines* of the early twentieth century; there could be examination, possibly even condemnation, of the materialistic woman who has her young lover-to-be (she was not aware of this at the time) trained for sexual prowess and talks about 'well-fed love'. There are many secondary characters, all brilliantly handled, and a use of sensory imagery, visual, tactile, olfactory in every field which has been analysed with imaginative yet scientific penetration by I. T. Olken of the University of Michigan. Here and there are signs that Colette used her own experience, even unconsciously, and as Chéri looks at the old photographs of Léa when young it is hard not to think of the author, who was approaching fifty as she wrote the book, remembering the portraits of herself when young, which are now collectors' items.

*Chéri* is almost a man, the one male creature in Colette's work, with the possible exception of Phil in *Le Blé en herbe,* who has an existence in his own right. The other men are subsidiary to the women, somehow faceless. But the genesis of Chéri is important in the consideration of Colette as an artist; she said nothing in her letters – those so far published – about the composition of the book, but wrote about it in a preface when it was published in her collected works in 1949. She described in detail a young man she had observed in 1911 and a character she had created, named 'Clouk'. The ugly Clouk gave way to the handsome Chéri but as Maurice Goudeket has pointed out in his important paper *Colette et l'art d'écrire,* neither of these young men had any roots. 'Léa is human, Chéri is barely so . . . The whole of *La Fin de Chéri* is no more than a long blind groping by Chéri towards a little human warmth, that is to say, for him, towards Léa. The drama of Chéri is that of the chrysalis.' Maurice Goudeket mentions Colette's obstinate search for communication between the world of humans and the world of animals and believes that in Chéri she may have personified her failure. This character and these two books preoccupied her for twenty-five years and whatever their qualities they represent the central point of her creative life.

A whole generation of Parisians have been inclined to accept Chéri merely as a portrait of Auguste Hériot amalgamated with memories of Henri de Jouvenel's sons, but these rumours are infinitely less valuable than the evidence of Colette's technical range supplied by these two novels.

If Proust had wept over *Mitsou,* André Gide, to his own surprise, deeply admired *Chéri* :

Madame,

I can wager that praise from me is praise which you hardly expect to receive. I myself am completely astonished that I should be writing to you, astonished at the great pleasure I have had in reading you. I have devoured *Chéri* at one go. What an admirable subject you have got hold of : and with what intelligence, what mastery, what understanding of the least confessed secrets of the body ! . . . From beginning to end of the book, there is not one weakness, not one redundancy, not one commonplace. At the most I was perhaps a little disappointed by the last pages; it was only up to you, it seems, to take the book higher, and the most difficult part of it was already done (this astonishing scene when he sees her again, perhaps the most successful in the whole book), after which the tirade of Chéri pleases me less than his silence would have done; and the reflections of Léa, her excuses : 'I have never spoken to you about the future . . .' it seems to me slightly less reasonable and restrictive. You explain what the reader understood without words.

What sureness of line ! what natural dialogue ! And the secondary characters, marvellous !

Why has no critic, as far as I know, thought of comparing your *Chéri* with the unbearable *Adolphe*; it is the other side of the same subject – almost.

But what I like most of all in your book, is what is cut out of it, and taken away from it, nudity.

I would like to read it again already – and I am afraid : if I should find it less good! Quickly, I will send this letter before putting it away.

Yours very attentively,<br>André Gide

Colette was famous, but she did not now take a rest because in the first place, as both her daughter and Maurice Goudeket assert, she never accepted that she was famous. She was usually pleased to keep the magazines in which her books were serialized, she seemed interested in reviews only when they condemned her utterly and she was forced to work without a break because she was perpetually in need of money. She had learned to value herself and once spoke lightly of her 'well-known cupidity'. When told once that she was asking more than Gide for a novel she remarked that Gide was obviously wrong.

Working with her friend the playwright Léopold Marchand Colette made *Chéri* into a play. She read it to Sidi who was 'very moved'. She described to her collaborator how she had re-written the end of the third act three times, 'grumbling and swearing'. After an attempt to use a 'film effect and silence' she had changed her mind and made her characters go on talking to the end. The performance in Paris late in 1921 was not however a great success, while at Lyons it was a 'disaster', for it had been under-rehearsed and badly publicized. However the co-authors were undeterred and went on to dramatize *La Vagabonde*.

In 1923 Colette published *Le Blé en Herbe*, which for some critics has offered competition to *Chéri* as Colette's masterpiece. Phil, who is sixteen, after receiving sexual initiation from a mature, solitary woman, takes the virginity of the fifteen-year-old Vinca, his holiday companion, whom he has loved for some time. The remarkable thing about the description of the sexual act, a phrase which seems inadequate, is the way in which Colette controlled its rhythm and speed. In 1923 the subject of the book seemed daring and serialization in *Le Matin* stopped because the directors would not subject the reading public to such a shock. A few years later Colette described her original conception of this book as theatrical. 'The story of this novel – the genesis, as you pedants say – is curious : for a long, long time I had wanted to write a one-act play for the Comédie-Française. ... The curtain rises, the stage is plunged in darkness, two invisible characters are talking about love with much knowledge and experience. As the dialogue ends the lights come on and the surprised spectators see that the partners are aged fifteen and sixten respectively. I wanted to show by this that passionate love has no age and that love does not have two types of language. ... In *Le Blé en herbe* this is all I have said. I have only added to the story a few landscapes of the Cancale district which had moved me **deeply.**'

Fifty years later the tone of the ending remains unrelated to any social convention; Phil looks at Vinca, who shows no emotion. 'A little sorrow, a little pleasure ... That's all I've given her ... that's all ...'. Reality, not morality, had preoccupied Colette. She was deeply preoccupied by 'the war between men and women' yet at this period of her life when her femininity had been so strong she seemed more successful at portraying men when they were young than when mature.

Her personal reality continued on the surface cheerfully enough; her daughter, whom she had named 'Bel-Gazou', a name adapted from words meaning 'fine speech', was growing up, the de Jouvenels and their friends gathered either at Castel-Novel or at Rozven. Sidi had become even more successful and in 1922 he was in charge of the French delegation attending the League of Nations conference on disarmament. Colette knew he had mistresses, including a well-known dress-designer, refers to them by name in her letters, with little comment, and was almost friendly towards them. She worked with superhuman energy in many fields, still writing for *Le Matin* and also choosing a series of novels to be published by Ferenczi, entitled 'Collection Colette'. She even embarked on an exhausting lecture tour in the South of France and the subject on which she had chosen to speak was 'The Problem of Life *à Deux*', but she decided, after writing her lecture, that she had better start again and talk about the theatre instead. Ironically enough she found herself billed in Bordeaux as 'Mademoiselle Colette de Jouvenel'. As she wrote to Marguerite Moreno, this was 'one way of pleasing everybody'. Sidi had developed a habit of disappearing and she did not always know where he was. He had asked her once why she could not write a book that was not about love, adultery or half-incestuous relationship; she was sorry that his 'amorous rendez-vous' left him no time to explain how one lived or wrote without love.

In October 1923 he was involved with 'a lady with horse-like bones who produces books in two volumes. He hasn't any luck, our Sidi. . . .' In early January 1924 Colette, writing from Auteuil, commiserated with Georges Wague's wife, who had matrimonial problems, and gave her practical advice. She added a postscript : 'I've been alone for a month. He left without a word while I was on a lecture tour. I'm divorcing.'

This was the year of the story-collection *La Femme Cachée* (inadequately translated perhaps as *The Secret Woman*), containing many vignettes of husband-wife situations. The stories 'prove' nothing, except that loving is difficult, and does not last long.

With two marriages behind her, each one lasting for a period of thirteen years, Colette was once again alone. Not quite, perhaps, for this time she had her daughter, Bel-Gazou, and her reputation as a writer. Also, she was about to prove the wisdom of her mother's prophecy, 'But you, what will you do with so many husbands? You get into the habit and then you can't manage without them.'

Henri de Jouvenel could not manage without a wife, and preferred a rich one. His new companion was a Dreyfus, who brought him useful connections with the Montefiore family. Colette was to remember this many years later and write a novel about it, *Julie de Carneilhan*. It is scarcely surprising that she referred to men in general as 'dear enemies'.

# 9

## *Close to Maurice*

If Colette was preoccupied with the possibility of communication
between the human and the animal kingdom, while watching
her many cats and various dogs, her squirrel and other creatures,
her findings about the alleged communication between people,
men and women, or women and women, are infinitely more
absorbing. The next fifteen years saw the composition of the
novels and non-fiction which, apart from *Chéri*, have most intrigued a discerning if divided public.

The background to this achievement was happiness, which
came with remarkable speed. She had been happy in 1912 and
for some time afterwards, but when the amiable strife of marriage had grown painful she became not bitter but resigned.
Colette, who had such strength within her, did not keep it for
jealous scenes but translated it into her work, into professional
and personal friendships, and her love for her daughter. After
her husband had moved away from her, becoming Minister of
State Education under the Poincaré government, she gave no
sign in her letters at least that she was incurably depressed or
conscious of failure and was delighted when 'Monsieur de
Jouvenel' gave her a small car; she described it as a 'Renaud',
no doubt thinking of her stepson. She went skiing with another
stepson, stayed with Marguerite Moreno in the south and decided

to face the theatre public again by appearing as Léa in the stage version of *Chéri*.

The play was produced at the Théâtre de Monte-Carlo in December 1924, with Moreno as Madame Peloux, and with the backing of Henri de Rothschild it came to Paris the following spring. Colette had not been seen on the stage for thirteen years, and in those days, before her second marriage, she had appeared principally as a mime. Those absurd dramas had entertained both her and the audiences, possibly for the wrong reasons. Acting was a more serious business, and strangely enough some of the best actresses in Paris had failed as Léa. Colette's friends advised that since she had created Léa she could surely interpret her better than anyone else. Léa had been elegant, and although Colette was striking to see and hear she was too short, too square, her neck was not long enough, her aggressively short hair was no longer sleek enough to enhance the shape of her face. Critics and journalists naturally gave the new Léa a good deal of attention : how could they resist such an opportunity? Opinions varied to an entertaining extent. 'Colette, you made me cry,' wrote the novelist Lucie Delarue-Mardrus. The cartoonist Vertès drew a portly Léa with a minute Chéri tucked under one arm. *La Revue de Paris* spoke earnestly of Colette's 'strange majesty, that of nature, an innocence without laws, that of animals, instinctive and maternal.' The critic even mentioned the value of her accent, 'bitter and rugged', while André Rouveyre again spared her nothing. He began by referring coldly to her earlier performances as a mime.

> Even today, [he wrote] she who handles the pen to the point of heartbreak is for us lifeless on the stage. In her headstrong attempts, she is, there before us, inferior even to herself. . . .
> She would appear childish alongside an intelligent professional actress. She speaks rather fast and in a way appar-

ently so detached from her partners, as though she was trying
to say : 'If you think I'm enjoying myself here among these
puppets. . . .' Colette vainly torments herself in an effort to
express her personal *daemon*.

He remains restive and cooped up. And she is like a stranger
who implores and deplores him. The work of Colette is a wild
fruit whose buds, flower and kernel escape the personal exhibition of Colette, even more than her Chéri escapes Léa. Colette
is carried away by life according to a dramatic contradiction.
Continually cast in the wake of her lively youth, and always
marked by the thumbprint of Willy, she has constantly tried
the most hazardous impulses, the most uncertain risqué pro-
jects; she remains inseparable from her youth and knocks her
head against it with an undiminished persistence. She has no
spontaneous means, no knack, and no art to express, as an
actress, the drama which she bears within herself. Or else,
perhaps, would it lodge uniformly in that little laugh with its
three nuances : ironic, fleeting, desperate – like an *ah! là là*,
it's not worth it . . .? That little laugh which she lets fall in
the middle of her interpretation – and of her life – rather
like the way Tom Thumb would scatter his pebbles on the
road . . . In any case, we shall remember that laugh as we
read *Chéri* again one day, or as we cut the pages of this new
book *La Fin de Chéri* that I have here. The strange laugh of
this provincial Colette lost in Paris, with her basket full of
beautiful peaches, grapes and strawberries; in Paris, where
she follows, with a goat-like brow, obstinate and hidden behind
a ramp of thick tangled hair, the timbre, the accent, the rather
awkward manners of an exile.

Although Rouveyre was writing no more than regular criticism
for a fortnightly review, he expressed here a good deal of
Colette's personality and the maladjustment which was at the

same time her strength. He recorded the piquancy of the situation; it did not touch him:

Let Madame Colette make no mistake: the spectator comes through curiosity about the writer's person. It is the legitimate response to her exhibitionist fantasy. Still, many readers have not been tempted by this satisfaction. There is a big gap between the number of those who enjoy her books and those who watch her acting. Let us say without embarrassment that the better of the two pleasures is precisely the more economical.

Colette was undeterred, mainly no doubt because she was preoccupied with so many other activities and events. During the winter of 1924–5, while staying with Marguerite Moreno, she had met, at the house of Madame Bloch-Levallois, a man rather younger than herself who lived in Paris where he worked as a *courtier en perles*, a broker in pearls. In letters written soon afterwards Colette describes how she met him again at Easter and he drove her back to Paris. She describes him as a 'classic Satan', enjoyed long talks with him, preferably at night, reported that she was delighted to find herself still earthbound. She wrote to her friend Hélène Picard, the poet: 'how incorrigible I am and how glad I am to be so!' Maurice Goudeket has written his own attractive account of this meeting. Colette remarked in a letter that happiness has no history. She told her friend Marguerite how things stood: '*Veux-tu savoir ce que c'est que le gars Maurice? C'est un salaud, et un ci et un ça, et même un chic type, et une peau de satin. C'est là que j'en suis.*' They lived, as biographers have said, happily ever after.

Against this background of love and companionship Colette achieved her greatest artistic successes but could scarcely be described as having 'settled down'. She continued to act in *Chéri*, which now went to the French provinces and into Belgium and Switzerland. Maurice Goudeket saw the performance and when questioned about Colette's acting he replied with entertaining honesty, 'Odd.' Her friend Léopold Marchand helped her to adapt *La Vagabonde* for the stage and one surviving photograph shows that if Colette in the 1920s made an odd Léa she made an even odder Renée Néré. She looked exactly like Colette, but Colette had not looked like Renée since 1910, when she had been younger, thinner, and, in this novel, so sad that she could hardly bear to speak of love. About the time when *La Vagabonde* was revived, with Paul Poiret, later better known as a couturier, playing the lead, the critic Albert Flament went to see Colette in her dressing-room in order to write a magazine profile of her. He found her to be 'the image of a woman painted by Renoir, with luscious arms – combing rapidly her short, thick hair, surrounding herself with a chestnut foam, like a sensual crest on a wave. . . . Eyes *made* for the stage, slanting upwards, and between their thick lashes, a look of youth, of *joie de vivre,* a spark of light so brilliant that it looks artificial. . . .'

In the meantime a very different and almost forgotten project was suddenly realized. The composer Ravel, whom she had known slightly when she was very young, had invited her some years earlier to compose the libretto for an opera but he had taken a long time to complete the music. *L'Enfant et les Sortilèges* was finally performed in Monte Carlo in the spring of 1925 and well received, but unfortunately a poor production destroyed it at the Comédie-Française in Paris the following year. During one of the most intriguing moments, the duet between the two cats, the audience added their own undisguised miaows. This delightful work, which was written by Colette when her daughter was young, reflects a child's reaction to magic and came into its own many years later. An ideal work for broadcasting, it has found international success in the world of opera.

In 1928 one of Colette's most remarkable books was published, *La Naissance du jour,* venerated in France and by some people outside it but dismissed by various non-French critics presumably because they are not interested in the background. One is reminded of Somerset Maugham's remark at the beginning of *The Razor's Edge* : 'If I call it a novel it is only because I don't know what else to call it. I have little story to tell and I end neither with a death nor a marriage.' Such 'story' as there is seems almost to obstruct the reader who can barely become interested in the girl who is in love with Vial. Vial himself is of secondary interest – like most of Colette's male characters – but he is in love with Colette. This unusual technique whereby 'Colette' appears in her own stories, first examined in detail by Elaine Marks, is on the whole successful, for one would rather she appeared honestly than thinly disguised. The other technical appeal of the book is due to the descriptions of the Saint-Tropez area where Colette, 'converted' to the South by Maurice Goudeket, had bought a house, 'La Treille Muscate', selling Rozven in Brittany after the many happy summers she had spent there. If Colette had known before how to handle colour while describing people and backgrounds, the vividness of the Mediterranean light helped her to develop the technique further and achieve some remarkable effects.

Other aspects of the book are more mysterious. The talks between Vial and the writer have been assumed to echo those between Maurice Goudeket and Colette, but he has denied this in his book *Près de Colette*, stating that the character of Vial was based on that of an antique-dealer whom the author had met. Each section of the book opens with a letter from Sido, which supplies the author with a 'text' on which she muses. These letters, which Colette quotes with such love and pride, may seem almost too good to be true, and Elaine Marks discovered that at least one of them had been 'arranged' and was much more literate and literary than the original, which was published in *Le Figaro Littéraire* in 1953. But if these letters were rewritten, does it matter? What mattered was the way in which Colette remembered her mother; accuracy, as in *La Maison de Claudine*, was of little importance.

If Colette's letters to her friends at the time seem youthful and energetic, how ironic is that famous statement : 'Love, one of the great commonplaces of existence, is withdrawing from mine.' It never in fact left her, it merely changed its nature, because she had changed; if she had found loving so difficult it was because she had expected too much and had also been afraid; she had wanted to give and take everything all at once. Now she understood the meaning of acceptance, and this, for her, was 'the break of day'. For over twenty years she had been writing about the discovery of herself, inevitably accompanied by the search for lost parents, for she could not really find herself until she had found them, especially Sido, who had haunted, perhaps dominated her. But in this book, where she seems to examine the pattern of her entire existence, Colette was the first to realize that even for herself she must remain *la femme cachée* : 'Do people imagine, in reading me, that I'm tracing my own portrait? Patience : it is only my model.'

This revealing book, which should obviously be read along with *La Maison de Claudine* of 1922 and *Sido* of 1929, was followed by a novel that was equally revealing, *La Seconde*. It has two heroines, Fanny, who is married to the successful playwright Farou, and Jane, his secretary. Jane is in love with Farou, and his young son is in love with Jane. Fanny discovers that Farou at least makes love to Jane, even if he does not love her. The situation is complicated by the relationship between the two women which seems more than mere friendship and is solved by Fanny's decision that she cannot handle Farou on her own. She needs, he needs, another woman there. It has been suggested that Colette was remembering in this novel, once described as a 'study in polygamy', her own toleration of Henri de Jouvenel's mistresses, but the value of this short book lies less in its autobiographical leads than in its artistry. Colette had always been a master of detail, and no book reveals that mastery more than *La Seconde,* with its 'clues' to emotional and physical states, its sensitive contrasting of the two women. Their attitude to men wryly echoes her own. 'They're timid, you know. ....' Fanny says 'And then, the way they are, whenever there is what we call a scene, or a quarrel, they immediately see the chance of getting rid of us forever. ....'

The theatrical background so dear to Colette is introduced here in a new way; the central figure – if that is the way to describe Farou – is a playwright, and the descriptions of how his plays are written, rehearsed and performed are masterly, full of movement, yet complete in a few sentences. Colette indulged her love of theatricality through the use of striking contrasts, but often on a minute scale. During a dress-rehearsal, for instance, when the atmosphere is highly charged, Jane slips out and brings Fanny a small bunch of violets. Jane needed to give, Fanny to receive, and something tangible was needed to express the curious link between them. It would be impossible to imagine a greater contrast than that between the dramatic artificiality of the theatre and the simplicity of the flowers, even though, as Jane says, they had no scent.

In 1946, when Colette wrote about her 'heroes' in one of her books of recollections, she considered that Farou was a more successful creation than the Maxime of *La Vagabonde* and the Jean of *L'Entrave*: '... I felt rather more at ease and my fine fellow was less artificial. Cosily ensconced between wife and mistress, Farou leans against both, acquiring a little life from two female rivals who do not hate each other. Who have not hated each other. Who will not hate each other. Who grow old with a high opinion of each other, without ever completely forgetting the contempt they had nursed for the man's peculiar cowardice. ... So-called *roman à clef*, how you tempt us! How you incite our pen, not to deny, but to establish the sentimental truth which binds two women and their tolerable unhappiness

in the service of one man!' At the end of her life Colette began
to look at several of her books again, usually with a critical eye.
However, if this story was a *roman à clef*, she gave no clue as to
the identity of her characters.

During the 1930s, a decade of extraordinary activity for Colette
in several fields, she published seven books which included three
novels, a collection of stories and two of her most illuminating
non-fiction titles. The earlier of these was *Ces Plaisirs* which was
re-titled definitively in 1941 as *Le Pur et l'impur*, a strange book
on several counts. The original title was an echo of something
she had written in *Le Blé en herbe*, 'those pleasures which are
lightly called physical', and the book itself was a series of recollections and musings on the theme of homosexuality, male
and female. A curious mixture of insecurity, concealed arrogance
and impatience made it impossible for Colette to put forward
theories or discuss ideas; her mental energy was absorbed in the
transmission of memories and tentative personal conclusions
through an allusive style where words and phrases carried
implications rather than meanings. *Le Pur et l'impur* contains intriguing anecdotes, such as a visit to an opium den, and discussions on the psychology of Don Juan, through the introduction
of a not-so-young playwright, now identified as the well-known
Henri Bernstein, and Edouard de Max, the actor of the 1890s
so brilliantly described by Cocteau. Marguerite Moreno appears,
there is a memorable portrait of Renée Vivien, the poet, and a
famous if only partially accurate account of the 'Ladies of
Llangollen'. The book is a striking example of Colette's impartiality concerning any aspect of sexual morality and provides
something of an answer to those tedious enquiries about her
'lesbianism'. When Cyril Connolly reviewed the English translation of the book in 1968 he mentioned that documentation about
lesbianism was hard to come by; about the state of *amitié
amoureuse*, such as that apparently experienced by Madame de
Staël and Juliette Récamier, much more is known, if only be-

cause it contains a cerebral element that leads at least one partner to write about it. This 'loving friendship' also embodies the essence of femininity, which is receptivity and warmth. 'Since Proust illuminated Sodom,' wrote Colette, 'we feel respect for what he wrote.' She goes on to say that his attempts to evoke Gomorrha are little more than entertaining. 'It is because, with all due respect to the imagination or mistaken idea of Proust, there is no Gomorrha.' The invisibly-patterned episodes in this book are more relevant to the personality of Colette than the gossip and anecdotes which have done her harm in the sense that they have probably prevented many people from reading her.

Although this is the most complex, the most important work of non-fiction Colette wrote, she was so uncertain about its title when working on it that she considered and rejected several, asking her friend Hélène Picard for advice. She had thought of *Remous* or *Ecumes*, remarking that the former was 'closer to the subject (or absence of subject)' while the latter was a more attractive word. At the same time she told Marguerite Moreno that one part of the book could be written as follows:

Les Unisexuelles

\*　　　\*　　　\*

Chapitre unique

\*　　　\*　　　\*

Il n'y a pas d'unisexuelles

\*　　　\*　　　\*

This was typical of the way she would shrug off her work when talking – for her letters are 'talked' rather than written – to friends.

During the early thirties in France too few people in fact read her books, or in any case she did not earn enough money from them to exist entirely on her literary earnings. In spite of her sound provincial upbringing she was not interested in living in a narrow, penny-pinching style. For her journalistic activity she sometimes needed to spend before she could earn, she could not live without a house in the country and in any case she was generous to herself and to others. In January 1931 she and Maurice Goudeket had moved into two adjacent apartments with two balconies on the top floor of the Hôtel Claridge in the Champs-Elysées. They had kept, at considerable expense, two separate front doors complete with separate doorbells. Colette thought the arrangement practical and referred to her 'perch' as a 'modest fairyland', a boat-deck, a little tower, a windmill; she enthused about the glittering stream of cars below on a rainy morning and described the cat's utter delight at her new home. Colette would have preferred to remain in the Palais-Royal, where she had had an *entresol* apartment for some time, but had been forced to leave it for health reasons. Practical the new arrangement might be, for Le Claridge was central and could provide various services; Colette could remain anonymous here if she wished, while only the friends she wanted to see could penetrate the hotel's defences. Missy came to see her, for example, and brought her 'a remarkable clip-on lamp'. But this was not the cheapest way to live. Colette was nearing sixty, she could only carry out the lecture tours and dramatic criticism she had taken on if her 'home' supplied her with some material comfort. She never forgot, throughout her whole life, that she and her family had been forced out of their home soon after her sixteenth birthday and the fear of poverty always haunted her – as it had Willy.

The depression in the United States had affected many aspects of life in Europe, and Maurice Goudeket suffered financially by what the French describe dramatically as *'le krach des perles'*. It was at this point that Colette, feeling that she needed more money than literature could produce – and how 'secure' after all was the book trade? – decided to put into practice an idea she had cherished for a long time. She had always believed that a writer who did nothing but write soon became an uninteresting and sterile person, and was herself never too proud or too dignified to take on anything, however strange, provided it was well-paid. But when she decided to launch a range of beauty products carrying her name, she was of course taking a risk. At the same time such a plan contained elements that had always appealed to her – the artistic use of cosmetics was essentially theatrical and she genuinely enjoyed the idea of seeing attractive women enhance their good looks. No woman, for her, was unattractive, but she often expressed in her articles amused criticism of their enslavement to fashion.

She had already discussed this idea with various people ten years earlier, but when André Maginot, a friend of Henri de Jouvenel, asked her soon after the First World War whether she still thought about it, she had replied, 'not often'. He encouraged her all the same, saying that 'the important thing is to try', and told her to write up over the door the words, 'I am called Colette and I sell scents'. In 1932 finance was found and the business was launched in the rue de Miromesnil, near the fashionable centre of Paris. 'A pretty shop', Maurice Goudeket, who was appointed manager, called it. It was more than that. It was extraordinary, with its white paint and shining nickel and the flowing signature 'Colette' across the front.

In order to counter – and make good use of – the surprise that this new departure caused, Colette wrote a gay and seemingly ingenuous article for the September number of *Vogue*, making out her action as the most natural thing in the world. Reading between the lines, it is evident that the artless way in which she mentions, then dismisses, the delicious back-to-nature treatments in store, results in not so much a justification but a very clever piece of copywriting any advertiser would do well to study. Here, the lessons of a hard-working life can be seen to be well-learned, and her business instincts well-developed. Women who came to stare out of curiosity, remained as paying clients.

She wrote:

The public has shown surprise – in my view, too much so – that from being a novelist I have turned into a manufacturer of products which enhance, create and preserve beauty. Not without a smile I look at my past, and I remember a time when people were surprised that from an idle and docile little wife I officially became a writer (I was only a writer in secret but for a good length of time). Barely had I justified my small fame as an author than I 'went on the boards' as they used to say. Like this I became a mime and something of a dancer and something of an acrobat, and already I underwent severe criticism : 'Why, you who . . . you whom . . . you whose gift for writing is no longer in question, you. . . .

Above this article, which was triumphantly entitled *Avatars*, was a wispy drawing by Vertès showing a nude Colette, draped only in a scarf flung about her shoulders, sitting on a dressing-room stool, looking with amusement at a performing poodle walking on its hindlegs and carrying a minute umbrella. A smaller drawing at the bottom of the page showed a writing desk, a comfortable chair and a small dog seated beside it. After a brief and dramatic description of her life up to date, Colette continued :

But now late in life I upset everything; now I manufacture and sell beauty products, now, at the age when others finish, I am presuming to begin. My case is serious. Friends criticise me, unknown people stop me in the street : 'Madame, is it true that you are opening, near the Place Beauveau, an Institute of which . . . a shop that . . .' I receive letters, some signed, others anonymous, which approve of me or disapprove of me, or question me, or make me realise the importance of a decision which I took without realising how serious it was

... Isn't it wonderful? I confess I am moved. It is true then that a writer is attached by strong links to a public which he does not know? The little schoolteacher from a distant village assures me : 'Madame, you have not the right to ...' but women of fifty beg me : 'Save me, make philtres, do miracles, save me, I've got wrinkles.'

How I love you, oh, my detractors, oh, my unknown advisers! Yet again I have to conquer you, I have to entrust myself to you yet again. Since the first time I put a poultice on the wrist of a little friend (we were both five years old) I assure you that I have made some progress, and changed my methods, for I used – oh, horror and disgust! – a living snail stuck on the cut and tied by the flat ribbons of a dandelion leaf ... but at the same remote epoch I already knew how to melt the cerate off a playing card, without burning the card, by using a candle flame. I learnt how to make rose vinegar, which cures chilblains, almost as well as my mother.

She mentioned other tempting secrets which were known to her.

A little later I learnt the mysteries of quince-water, so kind to the skin, quince-water which is made – don't tell anyone – from quinces. For thirty years I have practised the art of making cold cream as white as snow, smooth, resembling pure wax and rose water, and as for a certain pomade made from wool-grease, you won't make me say a word about it, nor about twenty other pieces of witchcraft either ...

Yes, once more I must show you what I can do. I have cheerfully decided to do so. I already find them beautiful, the women who are produced by my writer's hands, which are happy to touch the living, human substance whose colours they enliven and whose weaknesses they disguise. They are disinterested hands, and from now on they will be enlivened by a sort of maternal goodwill. . . .

And then, you wouldn't believe it, but women are naive. They have a childish ignorance about what suits their faces, a rather barbaric desire for colour, and at the same time a timid fear of not being like everybody else. They adopt a standard lipstick, accept a regulation ochre colour and insist on using cosmetics which make their eyelids greasy and shining, until they look as though they have eyes that perspire; they put on their rouge with a quick but uncertain hand, they put it too low, too near the nose, too far away from the eyes, or else in a hard circle. . . . . But I know so well what must be done with a woman's face, frightened, ageing, full of hope. I have looked at this wide landscape, the human visage, for so long that I travel through it without hesitation. How touching they are, and how proud they make me, the women whom I tend and improve, when they leave me impatiently to reach the light of the street, or the hard lights of evening. . . . From the threshold of my laboratory I look at them and I stop myself from calling after them : 'Go and please, go and love, go and do harm – go and play.'

Finally, a sketch of Colette in an overall, advising a 'client', and surrounded with chemical apparatus.

The little brochure listing the 'Colette' products is a fascinating document today, with references to theatrical make-up and a reminder not to neglect the inside of the mouth. Some of the names for lipsticks included 'Stolen Cherries', medium, and 'Tragic Red', dark, while a toning lotion was called 'Hop-Là'. Colette believed that kohl protected the eyes from strong light and ended her foreword to the catalogue by saying 'laugh, if you have cause to laugh. But do not cry or you will see your beauty leave you too soon.'

Colette was now on the threshold of sixty but her mass of

greying curly hair seemed more effervescent than ever, and if she still insisted on combing it over her high forehead – she seemed to feel guilty about this – she apparently had a capacity for remaining young. She tended to regard life as a succession of *jeunesses,* and perhaps the critic André Rouveyre had been right, she was so haunted by her own youth that she refused to grow old. There was severe competition in the beauty business in the thirties, especially since the British and American cosmetics companies had established themselves in Europe. So, in spite of all the publicity given to Colette's new venture, the shop in Paris and the 'subsidiaries' in Saint-Tropez and other places did not last long. Maurice Goudeket, who had realized from the outset that this business, even with hard work, would not earn a vast amount of money, has given an understanding description of Colette's attitude. She had hoped for a time that she might stop working, because every page was exhausting for her; but clients who came to Colette the 'beautician' brought books for Colette the writer to sign, 'proving that you cannot get rid of literature so easily'. And Maurice Goudeket may have remembered what Colette wrote about her 'prison' in the old days of the rue Jacob and the boulevard de Courcelles when she added : 'It is possible not to like something and yet acquire the habit of it, to cling to your enemies as much as to your friends.' This episode may have supplied her, he believed, with new themes and a new range of characters, for she had temporarily looked at a different world. She would sometimes complain 'if only I had a subject !' but one may wonder how genuine this complaint was.

The intensity of Colette's activity during the remaining years of the 1930s can also be judged from the four volumes of her letters which have been published so far. Since many of them explain in detail how lectures, theatre reviewing and other work had prevented her from writing sooner, it is remarkable that she wrote the letters at all. Addressed, with the exception of those to Wague, Léopold Marchand and one or two other professional acquaintances and collaborators, to her women friends, notably Moreno, Hélène Picard, the poet, and Renée Hamon, 'the little corsair', the letters are like barely interrupted talk but are fascinating for what they reveal of Colette. She greatly admired the poems of Hélène Picard, unknown outside France, and took a protective interest in the author, who lived alone and became ill. She encouraged her to work, as she did the younger Renée Hamon who was destined to die of cancer after writing at least one travel book of great interest. The fascination of the letters Colette wrote in later life is the energy they express, the affection and practical advice for women coping with problems more or less on their own. Among the invalids she visited was Meg Villars, the actress of English origin whom Willy had married; the two women had been close friends. Another constant theme is her struggle with the current book and with constant overwork. Literature is never discussed, authors are sometimes mentioned but their productions rarely.

Occasionally among the exchanges of news about health problems, travel or work organization there are a few valuable sentences about her own writing and the way she worked. In 1924 Marguerite Moreno was writing her memoirs, after earlier stories which Colette had published in *Le Matin*. While giving severe editorial advice Colette revealed some of her own secrets: 'Do you realize that in all this there isn't one word which *shows* the people you're talking about, or lets us *hear* them?' She advised a little dialogue, and 'No narration, good heavens! Detached touches and colours, and no need for a *conclusion*.' When describing a dinner she wanted 'a decor, and guests, and even dishes, it doesn't work otherwise!' She told Moreno to 'free herself' and to conceal the fact that she hated writing.

She hated it herself, or said she did, but wrote, as she told one of her friends, *pour assurer son été,* and wished she did not write with such painful slowness. On another occasion she mentioned that after one house-move work was her only chance to take a rest and early in 1933 she was 'scratching away' at a little novel, sometimes working eleven hours a day and complaining that work was very unhealthy.

This was *La Chatte,* published the same year, which was also the year when her ex-husband Henri de Jouvenel reached the height of his career on his appointment as French ambassador to Italy. Their daughter refused to go with him, Colette had to sort out family problems, write sub-titles for an American film and recover from a chest cold in order to demonstrate her beauty products in Nantes and La Rochelle. Maurice Goudeket was selling cheap washing-machines 'and a delightful tool for un-blocking water-pipes and lavatories' which Colette found to be 'a little masterpiece of ingenious good taste'. She christened it 'the ferret'. Colette had forced Claridges to reduce the rent of their two apartments and could say 'Enfin nous sommes *bien.*'

In the circumstances it was surprising that *La Chatte* was so good; it was brief, objective, with no wordage spent on descrip-tions, for Colette had apparently decided to deny herself this pleasure. For any reader interested in Colette's attempt to discover some communication betwen the human and animal world, this book is more rewarding than *Chéri.* Alain does not leave his young wife – who is not at all feminine – because he loves his cat Saha more, but because with Saha he can be himself. The relationship between the young man and the cat is one of the most acutely observed in all of Colette's fiction. The charac-ter of Alain can be said to support the belief of one French critic who has found that Colette's creation of young men – Chéri and Phil for example – is more satisfactory than that of men who are older and presumably mature. It is as though she preferred to write about men who had not yet moved too far from the potentially bisexual state of childhood and adolescence.

Later that year she found herself writing with such difficulty that she wondered if the cause was 'the beginning of impotence'. She told Hélène Picard that she would accept the situation cheerfully if she had any other means of livelihood. 'To live without writing, how marvellous!' Although these repeated remarks sound like a pose, Colette, who was now sixty, could justifiably feel fatigue after publishing about thirty books, in addition to all the other work she had done. As far as fiction was concerned she seems to have solved the problem by allowing herself, at last, a kind of self-indulgence.

*Duo* and its sequel *Le Toutounier* (1934 and 1939) are for the specialist, the addict. They represent what might even be called the 'decadence' of Colette, decadence only in the sense that she was now writing almost exclusively for her own enjoyment. That she did not enjoy the act of writing is well known, and she seems to have compensated for this by writing not about herself but in a sense for herself. These two novels illustrate perfectly the best and the least satisfactory aspects of Colette, and are set in a world of women. Alice, heroine of *Duo* and part-heroine of its sequel, is observed with immense care; every detail, from her fringed hairstyle to 'her little black armpits' and 'the beauty-spot . . . beside her navel' is described with seemingly detached yet somehow admiring precision. Her clothes, their colours, design and 'feel' are also dwelt on. Michel, her husband, is even less real than Colette's other male characters. The imaginative reader will succeed in 'seeing' him, but it is barely possible to believe in his jealousy, while his suicide seems irrelevant and fails to move us.

The starting-point of the story, the love-letter forgotten in the purple blotter, is not credible either. The blotter and the sunshine it reflects remain in the mind, glowing as if from a painting by Bonnard, but that Alice's casual lover should write such a letter – its banality at least seems 'right' – and that she should forget it, these facts could be classified as 'facts necessary for a story'. They do not seem inseparable from the characters of the protagonists. The development of the story is slow, the dénouement unconvincing. The 'addict' relishes the book because the author makes a virtuoso display of her talent for sensory evocation. She seems to be walking slowly round the garden and the countryside, noticing the crab-apple tree, the laburnum and the catalpa, enjoying the smell of the dining-room, the home-made honey, the succulent young guinea-fowl cooked with such care by the old servant Maria, who slowly came to take the heroine's side. It is Colette rather than Alice who absorbs, enjoys and records these sensations. By now Colette had detached herself from her women characters – she had always been detached from the men – but she used these women in the sense that through them she could see, hear, touch, feel, smell, in other words live round them rather than through them.

In *Duo* there had been references to Alice's three sisters, and in *Le Toutounier* Alice returns to the flat in Paris where two of them still live, the fourth being 'lost' as it were, making documentary films with her husband in the Pacific. In the earlier novel the Alice-Michel relationship fills the entire book, the servant Maria making occasional appearances. A good part of the novel lies in the description of Alice's appearance and her surroundings, while the reader must decide for himself most of what went on in Alice's mind. In *Le Toutounier* the existence of Alice and her sisters is filled in with details so telling that their entire background, characters and way of life acquire a vividness unparalleled in Colette's writing. The book is little more than a *conte* separated by five years from *Duo* but its richness is such that one feels Colette had thought about it while writing *Duo*, or even earlier. Some novelists with a liking for complicated plots might have attempted to combine both books in one, but Colette obviously preferred her readers to look more closely than would otherwise have been possible at three of the four Eudes daughters, and especially at Alice.

The apartment where the two unmarried sisters live is large, untidy and communal. Their father had taught music there, his pipe is still lying about among the papers on the desk. Their mother, significantly enough, is barely remembered. Clothes are shared, the glass ashtray has remained unbroken for thirty years. Alice, after Michel's death, comes home, finding the flat where she had lived with her husband intolerable to her, the country house is sold. The symbolism of her home-coming is almost over-emphasized, the central symbol being formed by the *toutounier* itself, the vast divan 'of English origin' where the sisters sleep. The term 'decadent' is only relevant here in the sense that Colette seems to have been overwhelmed, through the figure of Alice, by the need to reunite a family, even the absent sister, and bring them back from the unsatisfactory men in their lives to the only happiness, not this time the earthly paradise of a childhood home, but adolescence, early love affairs and the vague beginnings of an artistic career which each sister had pursued in a different field.

Colette also allowed herself the indirect expression of something that rarely occurs in her novels – violence. Her capacity for noticing, relishing, and expressing the physical world is one of the most highly developed aspects of her personality; her pre-occupation with the dramatic side of emotional and sexual life indicates a preoccupation which in other women might have become merely sensual. But this aspect of life never escaped the firm control of taste and intelligence. Colette was not afraid of violence – she had faced Charlotte Kinceler in the 1890s and 'la Panthère' in 1911. As a reporter she had confessed nervousness but always controlled it. Her heroines, however, rarely act with violence – their energy is expressed in a hundred other ways. But Hermine, in *Le Toutounier*, actually tries to shoot her lover's wife. The incident comes as something of a shock in Colette's work, but the shock is mitigated in three ways: the attempted *crime passionnel* is merely recounted after the event; fails because the gun did not go off, and 'Madame Weekend', Hermine's rival, is not only unmoved, she behaves with so much kind under-standing that the reader can almost laugh. The incident and

Colette's treatment of it seem to indicate an attempt to show that her characters were 'real' and could sometimes display aggression. Michel in *Duo* had already wilfully broken a vase and planned his suicide. But he was a man and by the end of *Le Toutounier* the reader is convinced that Colette, or rather the characters she created with such care, had become almost indifferent to men, either managed life without them or at least enjoyed pretending they did. Throughout Colette's fiction there are many implied criticisms of men, her heroines tolerate their behaviour and do not seem to expect much emotional return for the love they cannot prevent themselves from bestowing. Throughout *Duo* and *Le Toutounier* one cannot imagine that Alice had ever loved Michel : was there anything to love? But in the second novel there are several interchanges between the sisters which it would be tempting, if dangerous, to quote as Colette's views about men : 'Have you ever seen a man make a gesture at the precise moment when you expect him to do so?' 'The most difficult thing for a woman is to be certain of a man' : and Colombe at least could not permit love-making on the *toutounier* : 'Do that on the *toutounier*! I'd rather wear a chastity belt all my life! Our *toutounier,* it's so pure ...' Men in fact were unreliable and infinitely less valuable than women. In any case Colette could not resist giving these 'lines' to those attractive sisters.

The sisters are attractive – but much more so, one imagines, to women than to men. He would be a brave man who would tolerate such untidiness, such careless, casual living; he would be amused and even attracted, but he would not want to come too near or stay too long. In any case he would feel excluded. *Le Toutounier* is the true centre of what has been called the 'gynaeceum' of Colette. The four sisters are the essence, the final distillation of all the women, feminine women, whom Colette liked to watch : Minne, Mitsou, Fanny, Jane, later Julie de Carneilhan, and finally Gigi. Léa had been different, only partly feminine, possessing something of that masculinity found in any woman who controls a love affair. There was inevitably something of Colette in her, while Renée Néré had been almost exclusively Colette.

Four years had passed between the writing of these two novels and during that time Colette and her 'best friend', as she called Maurice Goudeket, had moved to 'an eagle's nest' high up on the Immeuble Marignan in the Champs-Elysées after the closure of Le Claridge. On 3rd April, 1935 they had been married at the Mairie of the 8th *arrondissement,* where the groom's birth had been recorded 'forty-five years earlier'. Colette wrote to Hélène Picard 'by the way, Maurice and I were married ten days or so ago. A ceremony of seventeen minutes inclusive, and two witnesses. . . . In a period of more than ten years we hadn't found a morning free for "regularization"!' Both she and her husband recounted later how they went out to Vaux-de-Cernay near Rambouillet to have lunch. This wedding breakfast 'comprised melting knuckles of pork, cooked in a casserole, dressed in their own pink lard and crackling, moistened with their gravy flavoured by a little celery, a little nutmeg, a little horse-radish, and all those wholesome vegetables which devote their aroma to their mistress meat. We had pancakes too. . . . Can one get married without champagne? Yes, if the champagne is made to retreat by one of those chance encounters that used to brighten our French inns, in the shape of an anonymous vintage, dark and golden as a Spanish shrine, which held its own with the pork and the cheese. . . .'

On the way back they drove through a snow-shower and Colette was so delighted by this unexpected 'manna' that she got out of the car and let the snowflakes fall on her face: 'what velvety snow!' she wrote some ten years later. 'It clung to the yellow catkins on the hazel-trees and fell so thickly that I begged my old friend, and new husband, to stop the car so that I might hear the snow whisper on the bed of dead leaves. It is a very gentle almost articulate, murmur. I've tried to describe it more than once. To compare it to the quiet praying of a crowd at worship is to fail once more, especially if I omit to mention that it is accompanied and accentuated by another rustling, like the diligent turning of silky pages. Beautiful April snow. ... The wild honeysuckle of Vaux-de-Cernay held it piled on its new little ears, and the water rushing from the springs was like the blue of a snake.'

Five months after this wedding Colette's daughter married a doctor but in October decided to divorce him for *un motif sans réplique: horreur physique.* In the first week of October Henri de Jouvenel had died from a clot of blood on the brain. Colette had not seen him for twelve years and said that she would not have recognized him in the street, for he had changed greatly. On being shown a recent photograph she had exclaimed 'Ah, he's lost.'

1935 was a crowded year and the new 'respectability' of marriage brought the couple invitations which apparently they would not otherwise have received. Colette and her husband were asked, along with many well-known people and journalists, to go to New York on the maiden voyage of the *Normandie,* the liner which at that time was the most splendid ever known, not only the biggest and fastest, but, so the shipping line hoped, the most luxurious and glamorous. Colette escaped from crowds and boredom by getting up at half-past five, the best time to see the ship, for she wanted to have it all to herself : 'No one in the blue swimming-pool, no one in the bar. The gymnasium offers ghostly athletes, a vaulting-horse, an inert bicycle, a camel-hump, a rowing machine – all that moves and rocks and bounds but remains motionless, teasing in silence the flexed muscle. All her lights ablaze, the *Normandie* offers a fête to the invisible.'

Her memories of this trip were published in *Mes Cahiers* in

1941 and she continued with her impressions of New York. One is reminded here of her dramatic criticism, for she concentrated on liking rather than on analysis : 'We do not easily submit to the ugliness of an architecture. On the other hand, we are eager to adopt what is beautiful. Beauty is the thing that most quickly ceases to astonish. After the first shock, the first, almost religious, thrill that strikes us dumb before New York seen from its port, we are happily at home with the harmony of its organ tones, its tiers, its giant termitaries pierced by sparkling eyes. An underground city will always excite our apprehension. But what more natural than for man to assault the sky? Throughout time he has scaled mountains, planned towers, coveted wings. His impetuosity is manifest here with an audacity so deliberate and so headstrong as to impose a style and engender an art.

'Singular observation : while the skyscrapers, seen from the *Normandie* through the warm mist, remain only blurred peaks, the largest for their vagueness, they resemble a grove of churches, a gothic bouquet, and remind us of that Catholic art that hurled its tapered arrow towards heaven, the steeple stretching up in aspiration.' She was reminded of the romantic cities 'that emerge, pennate and spiky, from the dreams of Gustave Doré, Victor Hugo, even Robida. All derived from the cube, faithful to the simple or multiplied quadrilateral.' Little else remains of Colette's brief visit to New York, apart from her discovery of Woolworths, a visit to Harlem and the well-worn anecdote about the cat : 'At last, someone who speaks French !'

Colette and her husband were photographed on the Empire State Building, Colette herself wearing sandals as she usually did and otherwise weighed down by the unflattering clothes of the period. After she had passed her thirties a hat invariably annihilated her, destroying the shape of her head, hiding the eyes that illuminated her face and drawing attention to her mouth which tended to look hard; the make-up fashionable at the time – *pace* her own taste and skill – hardly helped women of her age, and she, who so enjoyed describing women's faces and hair-styles, did not look at her best during her early sixties, at least for those who can only know her from photographs. Temporarily she had retired from the unconsciously well-staged personal appearance; private and professional life absorbed her, but her letters show that she felt exhausted and anxious. Her sixties and the 1930s in France continued in a state of quietly frenzied insecurity.

Colette occasionally had some dealings with the United States because there was talk about an adaptation of *Chéri* for Broadway and sometimes, with much grumbling, she would accept the writing of a scenario for projected films of American books, such as *Lac aux Dames* based on a novel by Vicki Baum. This particular scenario seems to have been lost.

These adaptations were written solely for money, for in spite of the public honours Colette now received, and the publication of documents like *Mes Apprentissages* in 1936, money was hard to come by. Maurice Goudeket began a novel and entered journalism, as he had always wanted to do. As Colette wrote the French sub-titles for the German film *Mädchen in Uniform* Germany was beginning to occupy more space in the newspapers. Colette herself had a highly gifted German language translator, the young Erna Redtenbacher, of Viennese origin, who at the time of the Anschluss decided she could no longer live in Austria. Colette introduced her to her young friend Renée Hamon saying 'Don't neglect poor Erna, her fate worries me'. This remark was later justified.

In September 1939, from the apartment in the Palais-Royal to which Colette had gratefully moved, following an admiring gesture from its previous owner, she wrote to one of her friends : 'I would never have believed that the human race would come to this a second time. . . .' She came to agree with Erna Redtenbacher that in wartime Paris was the only habitable place.

# 10

## *The Evening Star*

It was indeed a phoney war during which the concierge at 9 rue de Beaujolais, a Russian woman of good family, nearly died of malnutrition while Colette herself received oysters from her young friend Renée Hamon in Brittany. The concierge had tried to augment her income, since her husband's call-up, by taking commissions for hand-knitting; Colette tried to find her work and offered to advance money for buying the wool. She herself was busy, writing what she called 'harmless little articles', Maurice Goudeket wrote for *Match* and *Marie-Claire*, while they both gave talks for the French radio station Paris-Mondial which broadcast an overseas service. In early June, just before the German invasion, they were at their house at Méré, not far from Paris, by the 12th they were on their way to the ruined castle of Curemonte in the Corrèze district where Colette's daughter was living. Colette herself called it a 'verdant tomb' and wished sincerely she had stayed in Paris, but her husband had been anxious for her safety.

Curemonte consisted of twin castles built on a hill and gradually crumbling away, but the restored outbuildings provided room for several people. There was hardly any contact with the outside world and Colette received no letters for a month. One of the first she received brought her tragic news. Soon after the German occupation of the country Erna Redtenbacher had decided that she had no chance of survival. She had fallen in love with a young French girl, a friend of Renée Hamon, and they committed suicide together. Colette had felt anxious about her and she was deeply upset by this incident.

In her isolation she was still able to go for walks but had begun to suffer pain in her hip. An accident some years earlier had damaged her thigh bone, leading eventually to the arthritis which crippled her. There were few people to talk to and since there was nothing to do in Curemonte except work she began to write the recollections later entitled *Journal à Rebours*, enjoying the feeling, in spite of the depressing circumstances, that she was not writing to order. This book contains colourful descriptions of North Africa and Provence but is principally attractive for its passages about her childhood and the famous piece *La Chaufferette* (originally a radio talk) where she remembers her schooldays and describes how at the age of six she could read but did not want to write. 'No, I didn't want to write. When one can enter the enchanted kingdom of reading, why write? This repugnance which the act of writing inspired in me, was it not providential advice? It is rather late now to question myself about it. What is done is done. But in my youth I never, *never* wanted to write. No, I did not get up secretly at night to write verses with a pencil on the cover of a shoe-box! No, I did not utter inspired words to the west wind and the light of the moon!' She at least claimed that she was born not to write and never sent any 'promising' essays to any well-known writer. On the other hand, she received them constantly. 'I was then the only one of my sort, the only one born into the world in order not to write', she went on, protesting, it seems, too much, that she had thus been able to enjoy her childhood. It was too late now to stop writing and after forty-five years she had realized that French was a difficult language.

She hankered for Paris, where she was 'used to spending her wars'. 'Security,' she wrote to a friend, 'when it means total isola-

tion to a nauseating extent, I don't like it.' After a short stay at
Lyon petrol for the journey back was found, thanks perhaps to
a visit by Colette to her old friend Président Hériot, and to help
from the Swedish Consulate. Various letters and writings by
Colette and Maurice Goudeket's account in *Près de Colette* build
up a fragmented but vivid picture of Paris during the Occupation : the desperate and undignified search for food, Maurice
Goudeket's arrest and detention in prison at Compiègne, Colette's
anxious wait at home, talks with her neighbours in the Palais-
Royal, the man who kept canaries and refused to believe that
the Germans had occupied the city, the woman who had been
so badly treated while working for the temporary conquerors in
Germany. Léopold Marchand's wife, who had received so many
of the *Lettres de la Vagabonde*, killed herself because her
Polish-Jewish family had all 'disappeared'. Renée Hamon sent
Colette sacks of potatoes and strings of garlic from Brittany,
but Colette failed to find her any corn flakes in return. A polite
young German journalist who loved flowers came to pay his
respects to her.

It was a strange existence. Colette kept a small revolver at
hand but did not often leave her apartment. Her last works of
fiction were written and published during the Occupation, the
last novel, *Julie de Carneilhan*, appearing in 1941. In January
of that year Colette had written to Renée Hamon thanking her
for potatoes which were sweet and not floury, and for onions,
garlic, peas, bay leaves and the Jerusalem artichokes which everyone had begun to eat, after despising them earlier. It was cold,
she wrote, she hardly went out, she was not well. 'I've begun
*un semble-roman*, I don't know what to think about it, for I'm
getting on with unusual speed, not stopping to arrange flowers
suitably in vases, hang up little pictures and polish the silver.'
Winifred Bryher, the novelist, remembers seeing a copy in London
in 1944 and hearing that this expensive but more than welcome
short book had reached England via North Africa, three years

after publication. In style, but in style alone, the book seems related to *La Chatte*, for it is brief, uncluttered and bare of description. Curiously enough however Colette seems to have used her own personal experience of the early 1920s and written about the later and less happy years of her marriage to Henri de Jouvenel. Her heroine is the former wife of the attractive and successful Hubert d'Espivant, from whom she is now divorced because he wanted a wife who was richer and could help to further his career. Julie visits him while he is recovering from a sudden illness which might have been fatal and he tricks her into accepting a part in a complex financial deal involving his new wife. Had Julie not remembered how much she had once loved him she would not have done as he asked. Finally, in disgust and despair she returns not to any *toutounier* like the Eudes sisters but to the family château where her brother rears horses. This novel is the only one by Colette in which she writes not about the middle-class or the 'bourgeois bohemia' but about the aristocracy. Although there is little feeling in the book of emotional vindictiveness – the tone is one of constant understatement – the mere plot appears to be a cool retaliation in itself. Friends of Colette have even said that she should not have written *Julie*, but in a strange way it could be equated with *Mes Apprentissages*: her bitterness had to express itself somehow. In various books of reminiscences she admitted that jealousy had sometimes possessed her and brought out the violence in her nature. It has even been suggested that since Julie's initials, when reversed, are the same as those of Colette when she was Madame de Jouvenel, Julie obviously possesses some traits which belong also to her creator, but then few heroines of Colette are without them. Julie and Hubert's wife, Marianne, are as usual infinitely more interesting than the so-called 'hero', and one of the best scenes in the book is the confrontation between the former and the present Madame d'Espivant. D'Espivant himself may come of a reasonably good family but he behaves too dishonestly even to be called a cad, while his wife, whose background was related only to moneymaking, acts with courageous tact. This is one of the books which contain hints of what Colette felt about the abuse of social 'superiority'. There was never any doubt where her sympathies lay and if her criticism is implied rather than direct it is none the less severe for that.

As the war continued, Colette continued to write; the ever-increasing pain in her hip irritated her, caused her to experiment with many different kinds of treatment, from cycling in the Bois to new types of injection and led her to see that she might not be able to walk much longer. Since she was forced by the circumstances of war and bad health into a state of relative inactivity she was prevented for the first time in her life from trying to do too much, a factor which had surely affected her concentration in the past and caused so much grumbling. She used this enforced leisure to try out new techniques which seem to have appeared ready-perfected and yet did not upset the overall balance of the work in question. The most obvious example is the surrealist-type effect in *L'Enfant malade,* one of the four stories in *Le Képi,* published in 1943, the year of her seventieth birthday. The sick child, in his feverish dreams, thinks of words as by some free-association technique – *absinthe, abside, saint abside* – and as one French critic has pointed out, one inevitably recalls the extraordinary libretto written for Ravel before the war of 1914.

Colette wrote later that children and old people shared the same endurance, and without obstinate self-discipline she could surely not have written, just before *Le Képi,* the gayest, the most extrovert, of all her stories, *Gigi,* while her husband was in a prison camp. The happy ending, in which young love triumphs over the money-grubbing morality of kept women, is one reason for its success while another was the fact that 1900 was conveniently far away now and made the story into a period piece. At one level Colette may have 'forgotten' that the decade of her first marriage, *la Belle Epoque,* the 'gay nineties' in England, had receded into history for most people. For a young girl to be 'groomed' and trained in order to catch a rich lover the social background had to be a long way from 1941–2, and Colette, as she herself recorded, found her memory now played strange tricks with time. Cocteau, in his speech about Colette to the Belgian Academy in 1955 remarked that 'in order to focus, [her] internal vision . . . demanded a great distance'. He found that she would talk incessantly about the 'Claudine' period and appeared either to be unaware of the contemporary scene or else to regard it as unimportant.

The happy ending of *Gigi* was due less to a sudden escapism or a romantic wish to see love and innocence destroy the morality of the demi-monde but to the origin of the story : it was based on reality. Colette mentioned this but the full details were not published until after her death. There were in fact two stories behind *Gigi* – Colette's own recollections of how a group of 'survivors' from the age of Madame Peloux or earlier had told her, soon after the First World War, about a young girl who had been 'flighty' enough to refuse the usual 'arrangement' proposed to her by a rich admirer. Only the youngest of the mature ladies had insisted that the girl was right and so she was, for the admirer then offered marriage. In 1926 Paris and Deauville were highly excited by the romantic love match between an eighteen-year-old girl named Yola Henriquez, who was being trained as a singer, and the older Henri Letellier who was owner of *Le Journal,* the rival newspaper to *Le Matin.* Colette knew him and used his story, but it was so well-disguised that nobody in 1942 guessed its origin.

*Gigi,* which could be classified as a novella but not a novel, was published in that year by the revue *Présent* in Lyon, outside the occupied zone. The eighty-page tale was again published in Switzerland in 1943, while Christian Bérard illustrated one edition soon afterwards. By 1949 a hundred and thirty thousand copies of the story had been sold in France alone. Four years later when *Gigi* was to become a musical comedy on Broadway Colette herself caught sight of the young actress Audrey Hepburn during the film festival at Monte Carlo and said at once 'There is our Gigi for America.' Since then millions of people have enjoyed the story of Gigi without having heard of Colette or read a single one of her books. Six months before her death Colette watched, by means of a special television relay, the première of the stage adaptation at the Théâtre des Arts in Paris.

*Gigi* was the last work of fiction Colette wrote, although some quasi-fictional pieces have been published since her death. It was not however the end of writing or publishing. Reminiscences of various types, descriptive essays, a book about flowers, short texts for special occasions : eight more titles during her lifetime, two so far since her death and, up to 1972, five volumes of letters. Pierre Trahard, who admired her deeply, accused her of publishing too much, but when the fifteen volumes of her complete works were established after the war Maurice Goudeket reported that she rejected a great many texts as not good enough, in her opinion, for inclusion. If too much has been published to please the critics the general reader can at least browse and make his own choice, preferring perhaps to read about people Colette knew when she was young; actresses, writers, politicians, composers; or about embroidery, or amusing anecdotes from her days with *Le Matin*.

On the eve of the war in 1939 Colette had written to her friend the photographer Gisèle Freund wishing that she was still young. 'To be only fifty-eight. ... Then I was a happy and passionate woman.' By 1945 Colette may not have been any happier, because she now had apparently incurable arthritis, but she was famous. Her third husband has said that she was 'the least literary person' in the world, but the literary world insisted on her fame. She became the first woman member of the Académie Goncourt, after forty years of writing, and a few months after the end of the war Adrienne Monnier, bookshop owner, friend and acquaintance of so many celebrities, invited Colette to lunch with one of her friends and Paulette Gauthier-Villars, Willy's niece and the first woman professor of medicine in France. Shortly after her first divorce Madame Gauthier-Villars, then a small girl, had looked out of the window of a train and seen her 'aunt' standing on a railway platform. She was alone, she was the 'vagabond'. 'Aunt Colette! Aunt Colette!' the girl called out. But she was not allowed to speak to her aunt, who had been wicked enough to be divorced. Years later, during the 1930s, the same niece had noticed Colette rowing, alone, on the lake in the Bois de Boulogne. She waited for her to come ashore and after some hesitancy on Colette's part the two women were reconciled. Colette wrote to her niece later that she had found her at the edge of the lake 'like a little shell'.

In 1945, as the women walked down the rue de Babylone, everyone recognized Colette, everyone, especially girls on their way to a nearby lycée, turned to look at her. Adrienne Monnier looked closely at Colette. 'The beautiful, famous little triangular face is wonderfully similar to what it aways was. But how fierce is her glance! At first it is sharp, distrustful, as though for the stranger, the enemy; it becomes friendly slowly . . . and you are surprised all at once by feeling the warmth of a fine glance resting on you, like one which accompanies a gift.'

Colette hated snails and Adrienne Monnier was delighted for so did she; everyone had a garlicky hors d'oeuvre and then an omelette, for the restaurant had just received some fresh eggs. Meat was on the menu that day – it was still too soon after the end of the war for it to appear every day – so all four women enjoyed a chateaubriand. Colette admitted that she was not a serious meat-eater, *pas viandeuse,* she said, but liked vegetables, fruit and well-grilled things.

They talked of haunted houses and Colette remembered the one she had to leave because of 'hostile spirits'. She also mentioned a clairvoyante and later Adrienne Monnier asked if she could read Colette's hand, for she was curious to see it. 'The lines are very good. The head line on the left indicates a tendency to mysticism which has been overcome by reason. The mount of Venus is very much as one might expect, it shows a rich sensuality; with a mount like this one can communicate with all the things of this world. But the thumb, what an extraordinary thumb for a woman! What violence!

' "Madame Colette", I said to her, "you have a thumb like that of a pirate chief!"'

'She laughed.

' "It's true", she said. "I'm terribly violent, I've often felt like killing. I like knives, blades, not revolvers, they make a ridiculous noise, no, a silent blade, well sharpened. You don't realize, the handle is especially important, that's what you must rely on, it must fit your hand well, it has to have a hollow there, you have to take hold of it like this –" her fingers and her palm handled an imaginary blade but she made it visible, as the fakirs do.

' "Well", I said, "we're lucky that this splendid violence has gone into your art." '

The duality of Colette's nature comes through clearly in Adrienne Monnier's recollections: the intensity of her gaze, which in fact often frightened people, turning into friendly warmth. Nothing about her was tepid, nothing would lead her to compromise. At the end of her life she could barely bring herself to accept old age and physical pain, but she did so by accepting pain as a companion – her doctor-brother had regarded it as 'slightly venereal' – and age as an opportunity to write sometimes in a different way. Strain and struggle are absent from *L'Etoile Vesper* and *Le Fanal bleu,* secrets are given away and there is gossip of various sorts. But even if the writing became more relaxed Colette herself admitted that she could not escape *déformation professionelle*: 'I don't know when I shall succeed in not writing; the obsession, the compulsion date back half a century. The little finger of my right hand is somewhat bent because, when writing, the right hand supports itself on it like the kangaroo on its tail. Within me a tired mind continues with its gourmet's search, looks for a better word, and better than better.' At the end of her life she would ask Pauline, her servant, for writing paper, and when asked why she wanted to write she would reply that it was 'her job'. She tried to reconcile 'the habit of work and the commonsense desire to bring it to an end', but if in 1946 she could see 'the end of the road' she could still write in 1949, 'With humility, I am going to write again. There is no other destiny for me. But when does one stop writing? What warning is there? Does one's hand tremble? I thought in the past that the work of writing was like other tasks; the tool is laid down and one cries out in delight: "Finished!" and you clap your hands, from where there rain down grains of sand that one believed to be precious. ... It is then that you read in the outlines traced by the grains of sand the words: "To be continued ..."'

At the end of her life she looked back, as she had always done, wrote about her friends, her family, her brother Léo who died in 1940. When he last visited her he could not bear to think that strangers had taken over Saint-Sauveur. But she looked forward, in the sense that her curiosity never left her. She wrote, in a fragment published after her death, that she was becoming less afraid of sceptics and their judgement provided that they supplied her with her daily dose of astonishment. 'Shortage of money, which is relative, the absence of comfort, can be endured by means of pride. But not the need to be astonished. Astonish me, take trouble over it, I would not know how to manage without these last gleams of light.' Did she feel perhaps in those last years that her time for astonishing people was over?

# 11

## *Prisons and Paradise*

'She had been brought up in the country, and had now for the first time left it, and her manners revealed a strang combination of boldness and timidity. . . .'

These words might have been written about Colette in her twenties, but they were in fact written about George Sand by her lover Jules Sandeau. He continued, speaking of her 'secret uneasiness, and an ardour that ran to waste', of her 'richly endowed nature, stirring impatiently beneath the weight of a wealth not yet called into activity'. He spoke of a 'palpitating life' that seemed to move in her very hair.

The similarity seems extraordinary, especially when one remembers that George Sand was married at eighteen to a man ten years older than herself, decided after six years and the birth of two children that she could no longer tolerate marriage and came to Paris to earn her living. Unsure of what she wanted to do she found work with *Le Figaro* and was astonished when her novel *Indiana* was a success. Then, having found that writing earned her the money she constantly needed, she went on writing for the rest of her life. A comparison between Colette and George Sand is inevitable at a superficial level at least because no other French women writers have known such fame and been so closely identified with their own work.

Although France has been remarkably rich in creative activity

of all kinds there were not in the past a great number of outstanding women writers whose work has kept its interest and
value until today. Many centuries ago there were Louise Labé
and Marguerite de Navarre, both poets; then came Mademoiselle
de Scudéry and other *précieuses*; Madame de Lafayette, one of
the greatest classical writers, Madame de Sévigné, who has been
regarded as a 'classic' but was in no way classical. Then Madame
de Staël, highly intelligent but lacking in charm; George Sand;
Marceline Desbordes-Valmore, the elegiac poet; 'Gyp', the
Countess who laughed at her family and friends; Rachilde, who
is forgotten. Then, all at once, came Colette, the Comtesse de
Noailles and the Princesse Bibesco.

It is obvious from this brief list that in France, until 1900,
and to some extent afterwards, all women writers were members
of the aristocracy or like George Sand brought up by survivors
from the *ancien régime*. Women have always been valued in
France but only in relation to men, not in their own right. Only
France perhaps could have produced delightful and intelligent
women like Madame du Châtelet or Julie de Lespinasse, or the
organizers of salons, the writers of letters and journals who
formed such a civilized background for the activities of the
*encyclopédistes,* the changing literary scenes of the nineteenth
and early twentieth centuries. Women writers have achieved a
great deal in France, but secretly : Madame Arman de Caillavet
wrote the preface to *Les Plaisirs et les jours,* but Anatole France
signed it. In France there were no middle-class writers com-
parable to Jane Austen, the Brontës, George Eliot and many
other Victorian women novelists.

Strangely enough, therefore, Colette seems to have been the
first French woman writer who belonged uncompromisingly to
the middle class, and the provincial middle class at that. It is
here that the comparison with George Sand breaks down, for
Colette never had the dash and authoritative attitude of her
predecessor, *la dame de Nohant.* Colette was taught how to

write, and it was a long time before she dared speak with her own voice. George Sand had less training, if more education, and her 'collaboration' with Jules Sandeau was brief. Both writers affected men's clothes or manners for a time, one from romantic eccentricity combined with a wish to compete with men, the other from resignation and a temporary renouncement of men. A detailed examination of Colette's work as compared to that of George Sand would be interesting, but in order to have any value, the area of comparison would have to be strictly limited. Colette envied her predecessor, if only for the quantity of her production; ninety-six volumes without the supplement, which brings the number up to one hundred and nine.

'So many hours,' wrote Colette, 'stolen from travelling, idleness, reading, even from healthy feminine coquetry! How the devil did George Sand manage? That sturdy woman of letters found it possible to finish one novel and start another in the same hour. And she did not thereby lose either a lover or a puff of the narghile, not to mention [an autobiography] *Histoire de ma Vie* in twenty volumes, and I am overcome with astonishment. Forcefully, she managed her work, her curable sorrows, and her limited pleasures. I couldn't have done as much, and where she thought of the stacked barn I have lingered to contemplate the green flower of the corn. Mauriac consoles me with the biting praise : Where hasn't she foraged, this great bee?'

Colette seemed to be thinking of her own achievement as limited to a passive contemplation of detail. There was however much more to it than that, and the background against which she began to write is obviously relevant. She had reached Paris in 1893 when there was a dramatic contrast between the capital and the provinces. Women had no legal rights and very little opportunity to enter the professions but there was one method at that time, and it was available until 1914, by which women could achieve all the prestige and much of the status they wanted : they had to be actresses or theatrical performers of some kind. Actresses and *grandes cocottes* could enjoy themselves, earn money, and even if they were limited to crude methods they could usually hold their own in the war between men and women. Colette then, having experienced the dramatic 'translation' from the Puisaye to Paris, was made into a writer and found the spotlight on her first heroine, who was of course herself. Along with Polaire she also found herself in costume. She was in a sense an actress who worked with her pen. She protested later that she had never wanted to write, but write she did, for Willy, highly experienced in directing other people and used to the company of both writers and actresses, made her into an artificial creature. They had after all married because they found each other entertaining and spent most of their time together each acting a part. Willy had no doubt expected Collette to produce the artificial type of writing which he practised and which the public enjoyed. The whole mystery is here : the essence of the writing contained no obvious artifice at all.

Colette recorded that on her 'promotion' to a study of her own she was given a green shaded lamp. Thirty years later she wrote that 'without a lamp I can't concentrate'. When on her way to stay with a friend she wrote asking her, if there was no *lampe-à-travailler,* to buy one. The famous *fanal bleu,* the 'blue lantern' that gave its name to her last book of any length, made by fastening two sheets of the famous blue writing paper to a lamp shade, was the last spotlight. It illuminated the bedridden years when in her Palais-Royal apartment, reclining on her 'raft', surrounded by 'properties' such as the cases of butterflies, the glass paper-weights, always flowers and nearly until the end, the 'last cat', she was onstage for selected photographers, journalists and visitors.

Writers who became public figures tend to act a part when they have stopped writing; Colette was different inasmuch as she wrote all the time while acting the role for which she had been cast. The role of course was that of herself, and she never tired of it, for she had a great deal to discover. She found herself interesting and mysterious and perpetually tried to work out where her true self lay. From the very beginning her mother had hoped to make her into a reproduction of herself, her father had been given to fantasy, so had her husband. Happiness was difficult for loving was difficult, and loving was difficult for her because it was natural. There was little natural about her life until she was middle-aged. Since she found it hard to love or let herself be loved it was not surprising that she established personal relationships in artificial ways through barely disguised exhibitionism on the music-hall stage. She liked to look at herself, at photographs of herself. She, and the other women she enjoyed watching, were all actresses on a stage which changed as fashion changed; the spotlight of publicity glared down on her all her life, but protected as she was by careful *maquillage,* the physical emphasizing the mental, she did not flinch and continued to play her part.

Happiness was hard to find and hard to keep. Colette seemed not to trust it and she lacked confidence because her personality and work, for all the naturalness they showed on the surface, were not natural at all, they had been organized by methods of various kinds, some haphazard, some controlled, but in any case somehow artificial. This is perhaps partly the explanation of her 'amorality', her refusal or inability to see any distinction between what is usually called 'good' and 'bad'. She had grown up and matured among people who had eccentric or artificial ideas about social behaviour and morality generally. As a result she had no instinctive reaction for or against convention. Unconsciously she hid her confusion by remaining impartial, because she was perhaps unmoved.

Described by her third husband as 'the least literary person he had ever met', Colette read a great deal. She read only what she understood, just as she wrote only about what she knew. The French classics she knew well, and her theatrical criticism proves her detailed knowledge of seventeenth and eighteenth century drama. When she went to see one of these plays she usually read it again beforehand. She admired Zola's realism, Maupassant's quest for *le mot juste,* and above all Balzac. She rarely wrote directly about other writers but her closeness to Balzac is obvious. 'Balzac knew everything', she said. She too had found that people were inseparable from environment and the environment fascinated her for its own sake. She who continually moved house and spent little time in offices was still able to evoke them with a well-balanced amount of detail, and although her descriptions of landscapes and gardens have been much praised, her descriptions of buildings, usually containing a few specialist terms which baffle the translator, deserve special examination.

Among her contemporaries one of her favourites was Proust, whom she read, re-read and quoted. She was naturally fascinated by anyone so preoccupied, like herself, with the personal past and by the problems of the homosexual, whether conscious or not. Academic critics are now giving attention to these 'literary' aspects of Colette which have so far been neglected. Maurice Goudeket has described some of her other likes and dislikes, the latter including Dumas and the former some isolated works such as *Salammbô.* More interesting was her liking for all kinds of popular scientific works on subjects related to natural history. These books enabled her to absorb many strange facts about the outside world accompanied by a vocabulary of odd, baroque words. She travelled little outside France but relished especially as she grew older and more immobile travel books where reality mingled with fantasy. At the same time she enjoyed the chronicles of Stanley and Livingstone and of course the stories of Kipling.

Apart from her own experience, this was the literary background which contributed to her writing. She was highly intelligent but made few decisions on intellectual topics because within herself she was divided, a natural result of the unnatural background to her early life. At the end of her life she began to write freely about this and confessed her 'streak of virility'. For many years she had been insecure in many ways while the woman and the writer within her did not always exist on the same level. In her life she often seemed frivolous, tough and sexually orientated, while in her books there are constant undertones of sadness, desperate regret for her lost childhood, *pudeur*, which is more than 'modesty', all expressed in that haunting sentence 'I belong to a country I have abandoned'. She had left not only her village, and a family, but a whole way of life.

The country of ideas was not for her, instead she established her own *Carte de Tendre*, exploring the whole universe of sensation, impression and memory. All her skill was employed in the presentation and interweaving of the sensory image, in the evocation of the physical world and its effect upon the non-physical, that is, the minds of men and women. It was through this external world, about which her curiosity was infinite, that she reached the intangible. No person, animal or object is described through any abstraction or from a straightforward point of vantage, they become 'real' to the reader through some detail that can be seen, heard, touched or smelt. Sometimes this detail remains isolated, sometimes a mass of details are quietly built up into an extraordinary symphonic effect. The use of light and colour in *Chéri* is an obvious instance of this technique. Chéri knows that Léa is back in Paris because he sees the lamp shining 'like a mauve moon' while 'the bedroom lights filtered through the shutters, forming a golden comb'. At the same time there is a scent of lilac blossom in the air, a detail introduced without a hint of sentimentality a few lines later. One colour forms a background to the book – pink, the whole gamut of pink. Léa's salon is panelled in pink, the curtains are strawberry-coloured. Some shade of pink is mentioned on nearly every page and as though by some secret joke Léa's maid is called Rose.

This is only one example of one detailed area of Colette's

attainment. Other obvious ones include the vividness of her descriptive style, through which everything seen or felt remains natural and alive. She rarely described a scene that was motionless. Trees, leaves and flowers are vibrant with life and all the half-suspected living things which so often remain unnoticed come into the foreground. 'Close to my cheek, clinging to the trunk of the elm I lean against, sleeps a beautiful moth whose name I know: lycena. Closed up and elongated in a leaf-like shape, he awaits his hour. This evening, at sunset, tomorrow in the dew-soaked dawn, he will open his heavy wings with their stripes of yellow, grey and black.' This was Renée Néré in *L'Entrave*. She describes how the moth would fly away, 'showing two other smaller wings, brilliant, as red as a ripe cherry, streaked with black velvet. . . .' The observation is accurate but never dull or academic, for the moth remains alive, it is no decorative ornament.

Flowers and plants live in the same way; they too are a world of their own. Madame de Sévigné, who believed that 'naturalness' constituted the perfect style, had noticed, thinking no doubt of elms, that trees in early spring are red, not green, and Colette noticed the unexpected in the same way. It is difficult to select any one passage from *Pour un herbier*, so many are striking. 'Round the little sabot,' she wrote, describing an orchid, 'are five divergent arms, asymmetrical, green, spotted with brown. A fine lip with a white ground, shaped almost like the tongue of an iris, unfurls below them, stippled with violet, and recalls, yes, recalls the bag of an octopus; for in fact my orchid is an octopus: it possesses, if not the eight arms, the parrot-like beak of an octopod. . . .'

Her descriptions are all the more alive because every human sense is involved, especially the elusive sense of smell. The extent to which Colette can create an atmosphere and a state of mind by her evocations of perfumes and smells is a power which few writers share with her, for it is a power with strength but no crudeness. She does not necessarily describe or analyse the smells, she merely mentions them, and if the reader has no olfactory imagination it is his loss. When Renée Néré thought of her room in Paris the first detail which came to mind was 'the memory of the two-fold perfume which clings to the furnishings : English tobacco and jasmine that is slightly too sweet'.

Alice, in *Le Toutounier*, coming back alone to her sisters' flat after a long interval, notices before anything else that one of them must have changed her perfume. A later heroine, Julie, is reminded by the smell from a nearby fish-shop that she is forced to live in the wrong street.

Like animals, people can scent reactions between each other : 'At the same time there reached his nostrils' (this is Michel in *Duo*) 'the scent which revealed emotions, the sweat dragged cruelly out of the pores by fear, by anguish, the scent that caricatured the perfume of sandalwood, of heated boxwood, the perfume reserved for the hours of love and the long days of high summer.'

Other aspects of Colette's writing, some detailed, some much wider and involving construction of plot and character in addition to moral issues, await either discovery or analysis. Only one thing may escape analysis, just as happiness, love or beauty escape it, and that is, how these results were achieved, or, to be more precise, what makes an unconscious artist. However, Colette does not remain an important writer simply because the analysis of her imagery provides a rewarding literary or academic exercise. The imagery is one aspect of her extraordinary richness, and important precisely because it usually occupies its rightful place, supporting but not dominating the narrative, characters or theme. In the non-fiction the imagery is usually blended with memory into a unique fabric enjoyable for its own sake, often irrespective of subject matter. This is why so many prospective readers ask what a particular piece of writing is about, and why sometimes the only reply can be 'about Colette'. Colette invented herself through memory and observation, her stage-managers made her into a professional writer, for without someone at her side she might never have acquired confidence and come sufficiently to terms with reality to write and publish.

She rarely makes even a mention of any abstract conception – even *Le Pur et l'impur* contains only limited discursive passages between extended anecdotes – and she clearly enjoyed words for their own sake. She relished the sound of them and one hypothesis mentioned in France suggests that she might have preferred to be a composer rather than a writer. Her slowness in writing was due to a perfectionist search not only for the right word and the development of an image but for the harmony and balance of a sentence or a paragraph. Often she would work backwards from a word to a sensation or an 'idea', relying on the useful *Dictionnaire des idées suggérées par les mots* compiled by Paul Rouaix in 1921.

Colette, who had been young at a time when middle-class women were brought up solely to be efficient wives and mothers, received three honours which had never been granted to a woman in France before: the Grand Cross of the Legion of Honour, membership and presidency of the Académie Goncourt and a state funeral. Edmond de Goncourt had crabbily stated that no woman (and no Jew) were to be members of the Académie, but his wishes on both subjects were 'forgotten'. The Académie Française has not yet admitted a woman; Colette, when asked if she would value membership, would jokingly remark that she never visited gentlemen she did not know and in any case she could not see herself wearing a sword.

Writing by women, as distinct from women writers, has had a strange history in France. They were regarded during the nineteenth and early twentieth centuries not so much as writers but as purveyors of 'feminine' writing. Balzac had even told George Sand that she should write as a woman. 'You seek man such as he ought to be,' he wrote to her, 'I take him as he is . . . Idealize in what is pretty and fine, it's woman's work.' At the turn of the century several French critics found it entertaining to attack women who were hoping for some kind of emancipation. Some women such as 'Gérard d'Houville', daughter of José-Maria Hérédia and wife of Henri de Régnier, found it preferable to write under a masculine pseudonym. Gradually more and more women began to write and publish in France but they were hardly read outside their own country and it was not until after the second world war that French women became internationally famous as thinkers, critics, novelists of all types. Colette was the only woman writer in France to live through five decades of changing taste. Unlike many other women writers in all countries she never campaigned, never attacked or defended any cause of public interest. Her aggressive strength was used in describing the varying tensions in personal relationships, evoking the material world as she saw it, adding the descant of her memory, perfecting an instrument of style, resisting any attempt to make moral judgements. Others could write about politics, she limited herself to politicians and their styles of oratory. Some writers could discuss employment for women, she would describe the women she had seen working. Anything in the nature of feminism seemed absurd to her, results both practical and emotional could only be achieved, she felt, through the exercise of femininity. The masculine part of her mind would watch the feminine part at work, and in the discussions with 'mon amie Valentine' Colette reflected with amused impartiality on the women who thought they wanted 'reform' and 'freedom' but were not sure what these grand terms represented.

Women writers were free to attack the Church and moral codes if they wished, but Colette at least in her writing did no more than laugh indirectly at a pompous curé. As to 'good' and 'bad', since both existed, both could be written about. At the same time she was godmother to one of her secretaries who decided to enter the Church, and she herself would light candles in Notre-Dame des Victoires near the Palais-Royal when her young friend Renée Hamon was seriously ill.

A personal, subjective approach could obviously narrow the scope and value of a writer's work, but in the case of Colette it is combined with a range and style that harmonise with it and extend it into something unique. The bitter-sweet quality of her writing may come from the duality of her own nature : it is impossible to avoid this issue. There is a constant struggle between controlled aggression and a simultaneous need for freedom and submission. Loving had been difficult but the learning of it had produced her work. Woman or man? Colette and Willy had argued about it many years earlier and after she had once spoken about him to a journalist in 1926 Willy wrote to the review, *Les Nouvelles Littéraires* : 'In a light-hearted way the celebrated woman of letters tells our colleague that there was no bitterness in our literary disputes. I quote :

' "You are, Colette, the last of the lyric poets, you are too much of a man."

' "And you, Willy, you are too *chichi*, too much of a woman." '

The rôle of a classic is surely not to teach readers what to do or think, but to show them a personal vision of the world and generally to enrich their lives. By an extraordinary chain of events and sheer hard work this is what Colette achieved. The schoolgirl with the long plait, the actress in front of her mirror, the journalist, the professional novelist, the beautician, the old lady who still made up her face carefully and tried to conceal her high forehead beneath her grey, blue- or mauve-tinted curls : a succession of women who were one, each fascinating the other to such an extent that they – she – could live not in search of time lost, but outside it. And in so doing this composite, elusive woman, *la femme cachée* until the end, fascinates us.

Time could not be regained, the earthly paradise was lost. Colette, writing about it incessantly, knew that she would never find it again, no one ever does. 'I belong to a country I have abandoned.' The lost paradise cannot be replaced but the memory of it can provide strength to accept the emptiness that remains. When Colette composed *Prisons et paradis* in 1932 she wrote the title differently in one draft: *Prisons et solitudes*. Then she changed it. Unconsciously, perhaps, she knew that paradise and solitude were, strangely, sadly, inescapably identical.

In Saint-Sauveur the house where Colette was born is still there, with a plaque on the wall; the street has been re-named rue Colette, and the blue metal plate carries her signature in white, illegal, but achieved by local admirers through *force majeure*. In Châtillon-Coligny at the house from where she was married her initials and those of her fiancé can be seen carved on the window pane. In Paris there is still a gentlemen's outfitter on the left bank called 'Willy'. There is a plaque outside 9, rue de Beaujolais in the Palais-Royal, a silver engraved plaque in the Grand Véfour restaurant and adjacent to the Comédie-Française outside the gardens is the Place Colette. In a Marseille gallery is a delightful portrait by Moïse Kisling of Bel-Gazou, while Colette de Jouvenel, so like her father when young, now resembles her mother. All that Colette valued of her work is contained in the fifteen volumes which Maurice Goudeket helped her to establish. Colette would not accept the fact that she was famous. 'If I were famous,' she told her daughter, 'I would know.'

She did not admit to knowing herself. She led a crowded, dramatic, self-centred, loquacious, sometimes happy life but the highly-wrought, subjective work will last longer than the time it took to be written. The mystery of Colette's personality is illuminated not by what others have said about her but by what she wrote. Much more could be known about her but probably never will be. 'What Claudine has not said,' wrote one critic, 'we shall never know.' The two thousand or so letters she wrote to Sido were burnt by her elder brother, Achille Robineau-Duclos. The work is not easily related to that of anyone else for it is as solitary as she was, even with friends roundabout and husbands close by. Her mother, not long before she died, wrote to her daughter about one of her articles and remembered her as a girl, solitary except for a cat, the creature that she herself described as divine. 'I see, my dear,' [she wrote] 'that the old house and its garden haunt you. That pleases me and also makes me sad. I can still see your graceful little figure walking there, thinking of endless things: Mine-Belle following you quietly. Ah! if de Jouvenel had seen you at that time! How many memories come to mind! I see you when I think of you at that time more often in a pale blue dress which made you so pretty . . . How far away all that is. Yes, you were my golden sun. I used to tell you too that when you came into the room where I was, it grew lighter.'

# Chronology

1829    Birth of Jules-Joseph Colette, Colette's father, at Le Mourillon, Toulon.

1835    Birth of Adèle-Sidonie Landoy, Colette's mother, in the Boulevard Bonne Nouvelle, Paris.

1857    'Sido's first marriage, to Jules Robineau-Duclos, in Brussels. They live in the Puisaye, near Saint-Sauveur.

1859    Birth of Henri Gauthier-Villars, later known as 'Willy', in the Seine-et-Oise, near Paris.

1860    Birth of Sido's first child, Héloise-Emilie-Juliette. Captain Colette, invalided out of the army, comes to Saint-Sauveur to start work as a tax-collector.

1863    Birth of Sido's second child, Edmé-Jules-Achille.

1865    Death of Jules Robineau-Duclos.
        Sido's second marriage, to Captain Colette, in Saint-Sauveur, where they live in a house in the rue de l'Hospice.

1868    Birth of Léo Colette.

1873    Birth of Sidonie-Gabrielle Colette, 28th January.

1876    Birth of Henri de Jouvenel.

1880    Captain Colette retires.

1889    Birth of Maurice Goudeket, Paris.

1890    The Colette family, after financial ruin, leave Saint-Sauveur for the house of Doctor Achille Robineau-Duclos in Châtillon-sur-Loing (later Châtillon-Coligny) in the nearby Loiret district.

1891    Gabrielle Colette becomes engaged to Henri Gauthier-Villars, who called her simply 'Colette'.

1893    (May) They are married at Châtillon-sur-Loing, spend their honeymoon in the Jura and live in Paris, on the left bank : first at 28, then at 93, rue Jacob, and later at 177 bis, rue de Courcelles.

1900    Publication of *Claudine à l'école,* signed 'Willy'. On a brief visit to England Colette passes through London during the celebrations following the relief of Mafeking.

1902    A play based on *Claudine à Paris,* adapted by Willy and a colleague, produced at the Théâtre des Bouffes-Parisiens with the actress Polaire playing the lead.

1903    Colette receives her first lessons in the art of mime from Georges Wague.

        She collaborates with her husband in articles of musical criticism, called *Claudine au Concert.*

1904    Publication of *Dialogues de bêtes,* signed 'Colette Willy'.

1905    *Dialogues de bêtes* is enlarged, reprinted and prefaced by Francis Jammes.

        Death of Captain Colette.

1906    Colette and Willy are divorced. She goes to live at 44, rue de Villejust, often staying with the Marquise de Belboeuf ('Missy') at 2, rue Georges-Ville, near the Etoile, and in her villa at Le Crotoy on the Baie de Somme.

        She appears successfully as 'Pan' in the mime-drama *Paniska* at the Théâtre des Mathurins.

1907    (January) Colette and Missy appear in *Rêve d'Egypte* at the Moulin-Rouge. Their long kiss causes a violent scene.

(February) Colette stays with Renée Vivien, the poet, at Nice.

(November) She appears in the mime-drama *La Chair*. Publication of *La Retraite sentimentale,* the first novel signed 'Colette Willy'.

Letter to Francis Jammes saying that after her stage appearances she can no longer write to him, especially since she had played the parts of animals.

1908    Performs in mime-drama in the French provinces and in Belgium.

Appears as the heroine in her own stage version of *Claudine à Paris* in Brussels and Lyon.

Her half-sister Juliette hangs herself.

1909    Première of Colette's two-act play *En Camarades* at the Théâtre des Arts in Paris. Accompanied by her dog Toby-Chien, she plays the principal rôle herself.

The mime-drama *La Chair* performed at the Manhattan Opera House, New York, without Colette, who was disappointed because she could not go.

Willy sells the copyright of the *Claudine* titles outright to the original publishers, Ollendorff.

1909–10    Colette meets Henri de Jouvenel, co-editor of the newspaper *Le Matin,* and begins to contribute regular articles to it.

1910–11    Visits Naples and Nice with Auguste Hériot, then Tunis.

1911    Her novel *La Vagabonde* wins two votes from the Prix Goncourt jury.

She stays frequently at Rozven, the villa in Brittany which Missy had bought for her.

Missy is jealous of Henri de Jouvenel. Auguste Hériot begins a liaison with Henri de Jouvenel's former mistress.

1911–12     Tours France and Switzerland with Wague and Christine Kerf in the mime-drama *L'Oiseau de Nuit,* the title being adopted after a suggestion by Colette.

1912     Lives with Henry de Jouvenel in the rue Cortambert at Passy. Première, at the Bataclan music-hall, of *La Chatte Amoureuse,* a mime drama in which Colette was successful in the title rôle.

(September) Death of 'Sido'.

(December) Marries Henri de Jouvenel.

1913     (July) Birth of their daughter, Colette, at Castel-Novel, Varetz, in the Corrèze.

Death of Dr Robineau-Duclos in Paris.

1914     (October) Works as a voluntary night-nurse in Paris.

1914–15     (December to February) Goes to Verdun under a false name in order to be near her husband. She later published articles about her experiences.

1915–17     Various visits to Italy, including one to Venice; she writes descriptions which impress Proust.

1916     She takes over a small house on the Boulevard Suchet.

1917     A silent film of *La Vagabonde* is made in Italy.
Part of the manuscript of *Mitsou,* her first 'impersonal' novel, lost in the métro and re-written.

1919     First encounter with the writer Léopold Marchand with whom Colette later worked on the adaptation of various of her novels for the stage.

1920     Receives the *Légion d'honneur.*

1921     Première of the play *Chéri* (adapted with the help of Léopold Marchand) at the Théâtre Michel, Paris.

1922     Plays the part of Léa in *Chéri* at the request of the management, as the run comes to an end after about a hundred performances.

1923     Première of the play *La Vagabonde* (adapted with

the help of Léopold Marchand) at the Théâtre de la Renaissance, Paris.

Henri de Jouvenel goes to Geneva as a French delegate to the League of Nations.

1924    Colette divorces Henri de Jouvenel. Her work is now signed 'Colette'.

1925    Acts the rôle of Léa in *Chéri* at the Théâtre de la Renaissance in Paris and at the Théâtre du Parc in Brussels.

Meets Maurice Goudeket in the south of France (indirectly through Marguerite Moreno) and later lives with him in Paris.

Première of Ravel's opera *L'Enfant et les Sortilèges* (with libretto by Colette) at the Théâtre de Monte Carlo.

Henri de Jouvenel is appointed French High Commissioner in Syria, a post he leaves after a year.

1926    Colette buys the house La Treille Muscate near Saint-Tropez.

She acts in the stage adaptation of *La Vagabonde* in the south of France.

Moves to a ground floor apartment at 9, rue de Beaujolais in the Palais-Royal, where she lives until 1930.

1928    Colette is made an Officer of the *Légion d'honneur*.

1930    Is invited to Berlin, along with other writers, to see the Sarrasani travelling circus.

1931    Goes to live on the top floor of Le Claridge in the Champs-Elysées.

1932    With financial support from several eminent people, including the Pasha of Marrakesh and the Princesse de Polignac, Colette opens a beauty institute in the rue de Miromesnil, where beauty products bearing her name are sold. A subsidiary shop was opened in Saint-Tropez, but the venture was short-lived.

| | |
|---|---|
| 1933 | Gives at least thirty demonstrations in the art of make-up in French provincial towns. |
| | Writes the scenario for a film to be made by Marc Allégret, based on a novel by Vicki Baum and known in France as *Lac aux Dames.* |
| 1933–8 | Writes dramatic criticism for *Le Journal.* |
| 1934 | Writes a scenario for a film, *Divine,* directed by Max Ophuls. |
| 1935 | (April) Marries Maurice Goudeket in Paris. |
| | (May) Is invited with her husband to sail on the maiden voyage of the *Normandie* and to spend a few days in New York. |
| | (August) Marriage of Colette's daughter, followed by divorce. |
| | (October) Death of Henri de Jouvenel. |
| 1935 | Moves to the Immeuble Marignan in the Champs-Elysées. |
| 1936 | Received into the Belgian Royal Academy of Literature. |
| 1938 | Première of *Duo,* Colette's novel of 1934, adapted by Paul Géraldy, at the Théâtre Saint-Georges, Paris. |
| 1938 | Moves back to 9, rue de Beaujolais in the Palais-Royal, this time to an apartment above the one she had previously occupied. |
| 1940 | Death of Léo Colette. |
| | With her husband, leaves Paris following the German invasion of France and stays for a time with her daughter at Curemonte in the Corrèze. |
| 1941 | Returns to her Palais-Royal apartment in Paris. Arthritis in her hip gradually immobilizes her. |
| | Her husband is arrested and imprisoned for some time, after which he remains in the unoccupied zone. |

1942        Her last work of fiction, *Gigi,* is published in a
            periodical in Lyon.

1944        Colette hears that Missy, at 81, has tried to commit
            suicide.

1945        Colette is elected to the Académie Goncourt and later
            becomes their President.

1950        Première of the play *La Seconde,* adapted by Colette
            and Léopold Marchand from her novel of 1929, at
            the Théâtre de la Madeleine, Paris.

1953        Colette receives the Grand Cross of the *Légion
            d'honneur.* Première of the play *Le Ciel de lit,* a
            play by Jan de Hartog adapted for the stage by
            Colette, at the Théâtre de la Michodière, Paris.

1954        (August) Dies in her apartment at the Palais-Royal.
            She is given a state funeral, without the participation
            of the Church, and buried in the cemetery of Père-
            Lachaise.

# Bibliography

## (1) WORKS BY COLETTE

The following chronological list indicates the publishers (with locations and dates) of Colette's books. It has been compiled mainly from the bibliography established for the edition of the *Oeuvres complètes de Colette* of 1948–50 (see below). Various texts not included in the chronological list were published for the first time in these *Oeuvres complètes*.

Adaptations of books for the theatre and posthumous works have been listed separately.

*Claudine à l'école*, Paris : Ollendorff, 1900.

*Claudine à Paris*, Paris : Ollendorff, 1901.

*Claudine en ménage*, Paris : Mercure de France, 1902.

*Claudine s'en va*, Paris : Ollendorff, 1903.

*Minne*, Paris : Ollendorff, 1904.

*Les Egarements de Minne*, Paris : Ollendorff, 1905.

*Dialogues de bêtes*, Paris : Mercure de France, 1904.

*Sept Dialogues de bêtes.* Préface de Francis Jammes. Paris : Mercure de France, 1905.

*Le Retraite sentimentale*, Paris : Mercure de France, 1907.

*Les Vrilles de la vigne*, Paris : Editions de la Vie Parisienne, 1908.

*L'Ingénue libertine*, Paris : Ollendorff, 1909.

*La Vagabonde*, Paris : Ollendorff, 1911.

*L'Envers du Music-Hall*, Paris : Flammarion, 1913.

*L'Entrave*, Paris : Librairie des Lettres, 1913.

*Prrou, Poucette et quelques autres,* Paris : Librairie des Lettres, 1913.

*La Paix chez les bêtes,* Paris : Arthème Fayard, 1916. In part a new edition of the immediately preceding title.

*Les Heures longues 1914–17,* Paris : Arthème Fayard, 1917.

*Les Enfants dans les ruines,* Paris : Editions de la Maison du Livre, 1917.

*Dans la foule,* Paris : Editions Georges Crès et Cie., 1918.

*Mitsou ou Comment l'esprit vient aux filles,* Paris : Arthème Fayard, 1918.

*En camarades, pièce en deux actes* (included in the preceding volume).

*La Chambre éclairée,* Paris : Edouard Joseph, 1920.

*Chéri,* Paris : Arthème Fayard, 1920.

*La Maison de Claudine,* Paris : J. Ferenczi et fils, 1922.

*Le Voyage égoïste,* Paris : Editions d'art Edouard Pelletan, 1922.

*Le Blé en herbe,* Paris : Flammarion, 1923.

*Rêverie de nouvel an,* Paris : Stock, 1923.

*La Femme cachée,* Paris : Flammarion, 1924.

*Aventures quotidiennes,* Paris : Flammarion, 1924.

*Quatre Saisons,* Paris : Philippe Ortiz, 1925.

*L'Enfant et les sortilèges.* Musique de Maurice Ravel, Paris : Durand et Cie., 1925.

*La fin de Chéri,* Paris : Flammarion, 1926.

*La Naissance du jour,* Paris : Flammarion, 1928.

*Renée Vivien,* Abbeville : F. Paillart, 1928.

*La Seconde,* Paris : J. Ferenczi et fils, 1929.

*Sido,* Paris : Editions Krâ, 1929.

*Histoires pour Bel-Gazou,* Paris : Stock, 1930.

*Douze Dialogues de bêtes,* Paris : Mercure de France, 1930.

*Paradis terrestres,* Lausanne : Gonin et Cie., 1932.

*La Treille Muscate,* Paris : Aimé Jourde, 1932.

*Prisons et paradis,* Paris : J. Ferenczi et fils, 1932.

*Bibliography*

*Ces plaisirs* ..., Paris : J. Ferenczi et fils, 1932. (Title changed definitively to *Le Pur et l'impur* in 1941.)

*La Chatte*, Paris : Bernard Grasset, 1933.

*Duo*, Paris : J. Ferenczi et fils, 1934.

*La Jumelle noire*, Paris : J. Ferenczi et fils, 1934–8.

*Discours de réception à l'Académie Royale de Belgique*, Paris : Bernard Grasset, 1936.

*Mes Apprentissages*, Paris : J. Ferenczi et fils, 1936.

*Chats*, Paris : Jacques Nam, 1936.

*Splendeur des papillons*, Paris : Plon, 1937.

*Bella-Vista*, Paris : J. Ferenczi et fils, 1937.

*Le Toutounier*, Paris : J. Ferenczi et fils, 1939.

*Chambre d'hôtel*, Paris : Arthème Fayard, 1940.

*Mes Cahiers*, Paris : Aux Armes de Frances, 1941.

*Journal à rebours*, Paris : Arthème Fayard, 1941.

*Julie de Carneilhan*, Paris : Arthème Fayard, 1941.

*De ma fenêtre*, Paris : Aux Armes de France, 1942.

*De la patte à l'aile*, Paris : Corrêa, 1943.

*Flore et Pomone*, Paris : Editions de la Galerie Charpentier, 1943.

*Nudité*, Brussels : Editions de la Mappemonde, 1943.

*Le Képi*, Paris : Arthème Fayard, 1943.

*Broderie ancienne*, Monaco : Editions du Rocher, 1944.

*Gigi et autres nouvelles*, Lausanne : La Guilde du Livre, 1944.

*Trois...Six...Neuf...*, Paris : Corrêa, 1944.

*Belles Saisons*, Paris : Editions de la Galerie Charpentier, 1945.

*Une Amitié inattendue. Correspondance de Colette et de Francis Jammes. Introduction et notes de Robert Mallet*. Paris : Editions Emile-Paul frères, 1945.

*L'Etoile Vesper*, Geneva : Editions du Milieu de Monde, 1946.

*Pour un herbier*, Lausanne : Mermod, 1948.

*Trait pour trait*, Paris : Editions Le Fleuron, 1949.

*Journal intermittent*, Paris : Editions Le Fleuron, 1949.

*Le Fanal bleu*, Paris : J. Ferenczi et fils, 1949.

*La Fleur de l'âge*, Paris : Editions Le Fleuron, 1949.

*En Pays connu,* Paris : Editions Manuel Bruker, 1949.
*Chats de Colette,* Paris : Albin Michel, 1949.

## (2)   ADAPTATIONS OF BOOKS FOR THE STAGE

*Chéri, comédie en quatre acts,* par Colette et Léopold Marchand, Paris : Librairie Théâtrale, 1922.
*Le Ciel de lit,* comédie par Jan de Hartog. Adaptation française de Colette. Paris : France Illustration, 1953.
*Gigi. Adapté pour la scène par Colette et Anita Loos,* Paris : France Illustration, Supplément théâtral et littéraire, 1954.

## (3)   POSTHUMOUS WORKS

*Paysages et portraits,* Paris : Flammarion, 1958.
*Lettres à Hélène Picard,* Paris : Flammarion, 1958.
*Lettres à Marguerite Moréno,* Paris : Flammarion, 1959.
*Lettres de la vagabonde,* Paris : Flammarion, 1961.
*Lettres au petit Corsaire: Préface de Maurice Goudeket,* Paris : Flammarion, 1963.
*Contes des mille et un matins,* Paris : Flammarion, 1970.
*Lettres à ses pairs,* Paris : Flammarion, 1972.

## (4)   OEUVRES COMPLETES

Published by Le Fleuron, Flammarion, Paris, 1948–50.
When Colette went through her work for this definitive publication she rejected many texts, made several important changes and composed various prefaces. Some texts included in this edition had not been published before. Details of limited editions are given and in the last volume there is a bibliography of books and other writings about Colette up to June 1st 1950.

I  *Claudine à l'école, Claudine à Paris.*
II  *Claudine en ménage, Claudine s'en va, La Retraite sentimentale.*

III *L'Ingénue libertine, Les Vrilles de la vigne, Douze Dialogues de bêtes, Autres Bêtes.*

IV *La Vagabonde, l'Entrave, Dans la foule.*

V *L'Envers du Music-Hall, Mitsou, La Paix chez les bêtes, Les Heures longues, La Chambre éclairée.*

VI *Chéri, La Fin de Chéri, Le Voyage égoïste, Aventures quotidiennes.*

VII *La Maison de Claudine, Sido, Noces, Le Blé en herbe, La Femme cachée.*

VIII *La Naissance du jour, La Seconde, Prisons et paradis, Nudité.*

XI *Le Pur et l'impur, La Chatte, Duo, Le Toutounier, Belles Saisons.*

X *La Jumelle noire.*

XI *Mes Apprentissages, Bella-Vista, Chambre d'Hôtel, Julie de Carneilhan.*

XII *Journal à rebours, Le Képi, De ma fenêtre, Trois ... Six ... Neuf ...*

XIII *Gigi, L'Etoile Vesper, Mes Cahiers, Discours de réception.*

XIV *Le Fanal bleu, Pour un herbier, Trait pour trait, Journal intermittent, La Fleur de l'âge, En Pays connu, A portée de la main.*

XV *Théâtre: Chéri, La Vagabonde, En camarades, La Décapitée, L'Enfant et les sortilèges, Mélanges, Bibliographie.*

## (5) SELECT LIST OF BOOKS AND ARTICLES ABOUT COLETTE

Barney, Natalie Clifford, *Aventures de l'esprit*, Paris : Emile-Paule, 1929.

——, *Souvenirs indiscrets*, Paris : Flammarion, 1960.

Beaumont, Germaine, and Parinaud, André, *Colette par elle-même*, Paris : Editions du Seuil, 1951.

Beauvoir, Simone de, *Le Deuxième Sexe*, Paris : Gallimard, 1949.

Bonmariage, Sylvain, *Willy, Colette et moi*, Paris : Editions Charles Fremanger, 1954.

Champion, Pierre, *Marcel Schwob et son temps,* Paris : Grasset, 1927.

Chauvière, Claude, *Colette,* Paris : Firmin-Didot, 1931.

Cocteau, Jean, *Colette, Discours de réception à l'Académie Royale de langue et de littérature françaises de Belgique,* Paris : Grasset, 1955.

Davies, Margaret, *Colette,* London and Edinburgh : Oliver and Boyd, 1961.

Goudeket, Maurice, *Près de Colette,* Paris : Flammarion, 1956. *Close to Colette,* London : Secker and Warburg, 1957.

——, *La Douceur de Vieillir,* Paris : Flammarion, 1965. *The Delights of Growing Old,* London : Michael Joseph, 1967.

——, *Colette et l'art d'écrire, conférénce prononcée en avril 1959. Extraits des annales de la Faculté des Lettres et Sciences Humaines d'Aix,* tome 33.

Houssa, Nicole, *Le Souci de l'expression chez Colette, thèse,* Brussels : Palais des Académies, 1958.

Ketchum, Anne A., *Colette ou la naissance du jour – étude d'un malentendu,* Paris : Minard, 1968.

Larnac, Jean, *Colette, sa vie, son oeuvre,* Paris : Krâ, 1927.

Le Hardouin, Maria, *Colette,* Paris : Editions Universitaires, 1956.

Marks, Elaine, *Colette,* New Jersey : Rutgers University Press, 1960. London : Secker and Warburg, 1961.

Monnier, Adrienne, *Les Gazettes,* 1925–1945, Paris : Julliard, 1953.

Peyrefitte, Roger, *L'Exilé de Capri,* Paris : Flammarion, 1959.

Phelps, Robert (ed.), *Colette, Earthly Paradise,* an autobiography drawn from her lifetime writings, New York : Farrar, Strauss and Giroux, 1966. London : Secker and Warburg, 1966.

Raaphorst-Rousseau, Madeleine, *Colette, sa vie et son art,* Paris : Nizet, 1964.

Trahard, Pierre, *L'Art de Colette,* Paris : Jean Renard, 1941; Geneva : 1971.

Truc, Gonzague, *Madame Colette,* Paris : Corréa, 1941.

(6) PERIODICALS

*Bulletins de la Société des Amis de Colette en Puisaye,* 1–12, Saint-Sauveur-en-Puisaye : 1966–72.

## Bibliography

*Le Figaro,* Paris : various dates.

*Le Figaro littéraire,* Paris : various dates.

*French Studies,* 16, Oxford : Basil Blackwell, 1962.

Brigid Brophy, *New Statesman and Nation,* London : 9th August, 1963.

*Paris-Match,* Paris : various dates.

*Publications of the Modern Language Association,* LXXVII, New York : 1962.

Philippe Hériat, *La Revue de Paris,* Paris : September 1954.

*Studies in Philology,* LX, University of North Carolina Press, Chapel Hill : 1963.

Brigid Brophy, *The Sunday Times,* London : 16th April, 1967.

# Index

# *Index*

Book.. ..d be returned on or before the
last date stamped below.